THE HOME UNIVERSITY LIBRARY
OF MODERN KNOWLEDGE

CXCII

DIPLOMACY

DIPLOMACY

By

HAROLD NICOLSON

OXFORD UNIVERSITY PRESS
LONDON NEW YORK TORONTO

First published in 1939 and reprinted in 1939 (twice) and 1942

PRINTED IN GREAT BRITAIN

CONTENTS

THIS BOOK IS DEDICATED TO

HORACE RUMBOLD

AN IDEAL DIPLOMATIST

AUTHOR'S NOTE

SINCE this book was first published Nazi diplomacy has provoked the Second German War. It is no satisfaction for me to observe that my original analysis of the purposes and methods of German and Italian diplomacy has been so amply confirmed. It is, on the other hand, a great satisfaction to record that Mr. Anthony Eden has pledged himself to the fusion of the Consular and Diplomatic branches into one great Foreign Service. The details of Mr. Eden's scheme have not yet been elaborated, and the candidate for the Foreign Service should therefore regard as out of date the detailed prescriptions for application and entry set out in Section III of Chapter IX. He should apply to the Private Secretary at the Foreign Office for information as to the new regulations which will before long enter into force.

Apart from this, the comments and information contained in this book remain as valid as they were when it was first published.

H. N.

October 17th, 1941.

CHAPTER I

ORIGINS OF ORGANIZED DIPLOMACY

Since 1918 public opinion in democratic countries has become increasingly interested in foreign affairs—Their understanding of the problem has however been diminished owing to a confusion between " foreign policy " and " negotiation "—This confusion arises from the indiscriminate use of the word " diplomacy " as a term signifying many different things—The meaning of " diplomacy " as employed in this study—Origins of diplomatic practice—Prehistorical origins and taboos—The herald and his patron Hermes—The transition from the herald-diplomatist to the advocate-diplomatist—The Congress of Sparta in 432 B.C. as an illustration of diplomacy as organized by the Greek City States—The Romans and the conception of *ius naturale*—Byzantine diplomacy—The more scientific aspects of diplomacy as implied by the word " diploma " and its associations—The emergence in Italy of the art and profession of diplomacy—The transition between temporary and permanent embassies brings with it a change from the " orator " type of diplomatist to the " trained-observer " type—The confusion in diplomatic practice which existed before the nineteenth century—The regulations laid down by the Congresses of Vienna and Aix-la-Chapelle as the foundation of professional diplomacy—The practice of diplomacy is thereby consolidated and confirmed

IT will be useful, from the outset, to define what this book is about.

Before the war of 1914–18 the ordinary elector in Great Britain, in the Dominions and in the United States took but a spasmodic interest in international relations. There were periods, of course, when foreign policy became the subject of party, and even of platform, controversy. Yet for the most part the public were uninterested either in the principles of foreign policy or in the methods and agencies by and through which that policy was executed. There was the assumption that the foundations of foreign policy were based upon changeless national and imperial necessities and that, as such, they stood outside the arena of party conflict. There was a feeling that foreign affairs were a specialized and esoteric study, the secrets of which lay beyond the scope of the ordinary layman's experience or judgment. And there was thus a tendency to leave the conduct of foreign policy to the Cabinet and its attendant experts and to trust them to maintain national " rights and interests " by such methods, and by such combinations, as might appear to them at the time to be feasible and expedient.

Implicit in this state of public indifference was the confidence that successive Governments would do their utmost to preserve the greatest of all national interests, namely peace. And if a situation arose in which the vital liberties, rights, possessions or interests of the country were menaced by any threat of external force, the majority of the country would support the Government in its determination to resist that menace by the use of military and naval power.

The war of 1914–18 did much to change this negative or acquiescent attitude. On the one hand it was realized that a country might be committed (without its full knowledge, deliberation and approval) to policies involving definite pledges to foreign Powers. And that if a major crisis arose, the people might be faced overnight by the alternative of having either to repudiate promises which had been made in their name, or else to plunge into hostilities. On the other hand it was known that modern warfare is not confined in its effects to those professional soldiers and sailors who of their own free will have selected the profession of arms; but that it entails upon every individual citizen anxious ordeals, heavy anxieties and appalling dangers.

It was the realization of these two facts which, after the War, encouraged the ordinary elector in democratic countries to adopt towards international problems an attitude of less easy-going acquiescence, of better informed criticism, and of more continuous alertness. This was a valuable development. Yet in approaching this new, this intricate and this perplexing study, the mind of the general public became confused. Their alertness took the form of anxiety; their criticism manifested itself all too often in shapes of exaggerated suspicion ; and their attention became strained.

One of the main causes of this anxious bewilderment was the mistake made by the public in confusing *policy* with *negotiation* and in calling the two branches of their subject by the same ill-favoured name of "Diplomacy." They failed to distinguish between what might be called the "legislative" aspect of the problem and what might be called its "executive" aspect. For whereas "foreign policy" in democratic countries should be a matter for the Cabinet to decide with the approval of the elected representatives of the people ; the execution of that policy, whether we call it "diplomacy" or "negotiation," should generally be left to professionals of experience and discretion.

This distinction is in fact vital to any sound democratic control of foreign policy. In domestic affairs, in which the public have the accumulated experience of many generations, the distinction causes no difficulty. A budget or an education bill is framed by the responsible Minister in consultation with his departmental experts ; it is then discussed by the Cabinet as a whole and submitted to Parliament for deliberation and decision ; and thereafter it is handed over to the executive for execution. Public interest is rightly focused upon the early deliberative stages during which the " policy " is being framed and decided; the subsequent " executive stage," during which it is being carried out, affects them less immediately. In foreign affairs, however, the electorate have not as yet acquired the habit of making this convenient distinction; and their failure to acquire this habit is largely due to the continuous misuse of this word " diplomacy " as implying both the framing of foreign policy and its execution.

It is thus essential, at the outset of this study, to define what the word " diplomacy " really means and in what sense, or senses, it will be used in the pages that follow.

II

In current language this word " diplomacy " is carelessly taken to denote several quite different things. At one moment it is employed as a synonym for " foreign policy," as when we say " British diplomacy in the Near East has been lacking in vigour." At another moment it signifies " negotiation," as when we say " the problem is one which might well be solved by diplomacy." More specifically, the word denotes the processes and machinery by which such negotiation is carried out. A fourth meaning is that of a branch of the Foreign Service, as when one says " my nephew is working for diplomacy." And a fifth interpretation which this unfortunate word is made to carry is that of an abstract quality or gift, which, in its best sense, implies skill in the conduct of international negotiation; and, in its worst sense, implies the more guileful aspects of tact.

These five interpretations are, in English-speaking countries, used indiscriminately, with the result that there are few branches of politics which have been exposed to such confusion of thought. If, for instance, the word "army" were used to mean the exercise of power, the art of strategy, the science of tactics, the profession of a soldier and the combative instincts of man—we should expect public discussion on military matters to lead to much misunderstanding.

The purpose of this monograph is to describe, in simple but precise forms, what diplomacy is and what it is not. In the first two chapters a short sketch will be given of the origins and evolution of diplomatic practice and theory. The purpose of this historical review will be to show that diplomacy is neither the invention nor the pastime of some particular political system, but is an essential element in any reasonable relation between man and man and between nation and nation. An examination will follow of recent modifications in diplomatic methods, with special reference to the problems of "open" and "secret" diplomacy and to the difficulty of combining efficient diplomacy with democratic control. Other sections will deal with the actual functioning of modern diplomacy, with the relation between diplomacy and commerce, with the organization and administration of the Foreign Service, with diplomacy by Conference and with the League of Nations as an instrument of negotiation. At the end a reasoned catalogue will be given of current diplomatic phrases such as may assist the student in understanding the technical language (it is something more than mere jargon) which diplomacy has evolved.

Yet before embarking upon so wide a field of examination, it is, as has been said, necessary to define in what sense, or senses, the word " diplomacy " will be used in this study. I propose to employ the definition given by the Oxford English Dictionary. It is as follows:

" Diplomacy is the management of international relations by negotiation; the method by which these relations are adjusted and managed by ambassadors and envoys; the business or art of the diplomatist."

By taking this precise, although wide, definition as my terms of reference I hope to avoid straying, on the one hand into the sands of foreign policy, and on the other into the marshes of international law. I shall discuss the several policies or systems of the different nations only in so far as they affect the methods by which, and the standards according to which, such policies are carried out. I shall mention international law only in so far as it advances diplomatic theory or affects the privileges, immunities, and actions of diplomatic envoys. And I shall thus hope to be able to concentrate upon the "executive" rather than upon the "legislative" aspects of the problem.

III

It is first necessary to consider how and why diplomatic practice arose in human society.

I am conscious that the expression "diplomatic practice" may in itself give rise to that ambiguity which I have just deplored. By some it may be interpreted as signifying those habits of conducting international business which, after centuries of experience, diplomatists have found to be the most efficient: by others it may be taken as denoting those principles of negotiation which are common to all international intercourse and as such independent of transitory changes in systems of government or in foreign policy.

It will be well, therefore, to keep these two shades of interpretation distinct from each other. In the present chapter I shall examine by what stages men came to invent and develop the actual machinery of a professional diplomatic service. In my next chapter I shall examine how the general conception and rules of the art of negotiation emerged as something essentially different from (although always supplementary and even subservient to) state-craft on the one hand and politics upon the other. I shall therefore begin with the origins and evolution of the diplomatic service.

Diplomacy, in the sense of the ordered conduct of relations between one group of human beings and another group alien to themselves, is far older than history. The theorists of the sixteenth century contended that the first diplomatists were angels, in that they served as " angeloi " or messengers between heaven and earth. This is not a view which would be held by modern historians.

Even in pre-history there must have come moments when one group of savages wished to negotiate with another group of savages, if only for the purpose of indicating that they had had enough of the day's battle and would like a pause in which to collect their wounded and to bury their dead. From the very first, even to our Cromagnon or Neanderthal ancestors, it must have become apparent that such negotiations would be severely hampered if the emissary from one side were killed and eaten by the other side before he had had time to deliver his message. The practice must therefore have become established even in the remotest times that it would be better to grant to such negotiators certain privileges and immunities which were denied to warriors. The persons of such envoys or messengers, if properly accredited, must from the first have been regarded as in some way "sacrosanct"; and from this practice derive those special immunities and privileges enjoyed by diplomatists to-day.

It must be remembered that in primitive society all foreigners were regarded as both dangerous and impure. When Justin II sent ambassadors to negotiate with the Seljuk Turks they were first subjected to purification for the purpose of exorcising all harmful influence. The tribal wizards danced round them in a frenzy of ecstasy burning incense, beating tambourines and endeavouring by all known magic to mitigate the dangers of infection. Envoys to the Tartar Khans were also obliged to pass through fire before they could be allowed into the presence, and even the gifts which they had brought with them were similarly sterilized. So late as the fifteenth century the Republic of Venice threatened with banishment, or even death, those Venetians who held intercourse with any member of a foreign legation. Even to-day some relics of this taboo can be detected in Moscow and in Teheran. In London, and other more advanced capitals, the process of purification to which foreign ambassadors are subjected is more gradual and less overt.

In antiquity, this taboo against foreigners and

especially against foreign envoys was widespread and potent. In order to mitigate its severity the practice arose of assigning diplomatic privileges to a special functionary, namely the tribal, or city, herald. These heralds were invested with semi-religious authority and placed under the special tutelage of the God Hermes. The choice of this deity had an unfortunate effect upon the subsequent repute of the Diplomatic Service.

The God Hermes, it will be remembered, symbolized for the ancients the qualities of charm, trickery and cunning. On the very day of his birth he stole fifty head of cattle from his brother Apollo, and then (having hidden the cows in a cave) returned to sleep peacefully in his cradle. This resourcefulness on his part was warmly applauded by Zeus who thereafter employed Hermes upon the most delicate diplomatic missions, including the murder of Argos. By the Greeks Hermes was regarded as the kindly but unscrupulous patron of travellers, merchants and thieves. It was he who endowed Pandora, the first woman, with the gift of flattery and deception. It was from him that the heralds derived the strength of their voice and the retentiveness of their memory. He came to be regarded as the intermediary between the upper and the lower worlds; yet although he was widely popular, he was not deeply respected. Later diplomatists have often regretted that someone less brilliant but more reliable was not chosen as their tutelar deity.

IV

When we pass from the mythological to the historical, we find ourselves upon surer and more reputable ground. The heralds of the Homeric period were not only the accredited agents of negotiation, but were also charged with the functions of managing the royal household, keeping order at assemblies and conducting certain religious rites. As Greek civilization developed, and as relations between the several city states became at once closer and more competitive, it was found that the art of negotiation entailed qualities of a higher level than those possessed by the town-crier. The profession of herald often ran in families, and the main qualification for an efficient herald was that he should possess a retentive memory and a very loud voice. With the increasing complexity of the commercial and political relations between the several city states it became necessary to raise the standard of this rudimentary diplomatic service.

The Greek city states from the sixth century onwards adopted the practice of choosing as their Ambassadors the finest orators, the most plausible forensic advocates, that the community could produce. The task of these envoys was to plead the cause of their city before the popular assemblies of foreign leagues or cities. They were not expected to acquire information regarding the countries which they visited or to write any reports on their return; all that was expected of them was that they should make a magnificent speech.

Readers of Thucydides will recall how magnificent, and how long, such speeches were. They will also have observed that in the course of the fifth century B.C. these special missions between the Greek city states had become so frequent that something approaching our own system of regular diplomatic intercourse had been achieved.

Thucydides, in the opening chapters of his history, gives us a full and instructive account of the nature and procedure of a Greek diplomatic conference. He describes how the Spartans summoned a conference of their allies for the purpose of deciding whether Athens had in fact violated her treaties and whether she should be punished by war. This conference took place at Sparta in 432 B.C. Thucydides' record provides us with much valuable information regarding Greek diplomatic practice.

In the first place, there was the question of procedure. The delegations from Megara and Corinth made long speeches to the Lacedaemonian Assembly in which they outlined their case against Athens. They were then asked to withdraw and the Assembly debated what action should be taken. A motion in favour of war was put to the vote and was carried, first by acclamation and then by a numerical count.

The second point which emerges from Thucydides' record is that an Athenian delegation happened to be present in Sparta at the time. This delegation had not been invited to the Conference, which was composed solely of members of the Peloponnesian League. They were there " on some other business," probably in connection with some trade treaty. Yet they were not only allowed to attend the discussions of their impending enemies but were also permitted to intervene in the debate. And even when the League had voted for war against Athens, this Athenian trade-delegation were allowed to remain on in Sparta until their own special business had been despatched. This shows that the general diplomatic practice of the city states was unexpectedly advanced.

Thucydides' record of the Sparta Conference indicates that by the fifth century the Greeks had elaborated some system of constant diplomatic relations; that members of diplomatic missions were accorded certain immunities and great consideration; and that it had come to be recognized that the relations between states could not be managed or adjusted merely by ruse and violence, and that there was some implicit " law " which was above immediate national interests or momentary expediency.

V

These traditions and these precepts were handed down from the Greeks to the Romans. The latter were not gifted with any special aptitude for the art of negotiation and during the many centuries of their supremacy their methods were those of the legionary and the road-maker rather than those of the diplomatist. At the worst, they were ruthless in their objectives and brutal in their methods. At the best, they evolved the principle of crushing their more obstinate opponents and sparing the submissive. The Roman contribution to diplomacy is to be sought for, not in the area of negotiation, but in the area of international law.

It would be far beyond the scope of this monograph to enter into a discussion of the difference between *ius civile* (the law as it applied as between Roman citizens) and *ius gentium* (the law as it applied between citizens and foreigners) and *ius naturale* (the law that is common to all mankind). The Roman doctrine of the validity of contracts naturally entailed a firm belief in the sanctity of treaties, and the popularity of the Regulus legend (the story of the man who sacrificed his life rather than break his pledge to the Carthaginians) shows that this conception was deeply rooted in the

Roman conscience. The vague idea of a *ius naturale* did, moreover, imply a conception of certain principles of what we should now call international conduct. It suggested a fundamental idea of " right " applicable to all races and in all circumstances. It laid stress upon the duty of faithfulness to engagements. And it taught that the interpretation of treaties must be based, not upon the mere letter of the bond, but upon considerations of equity and reason.

Valuable, and indeed vital, as these contributions were, they were contributions rather to the theory of diplomacy than to its practice. The Roman system did, as will be seen later, create the profession of trained archivists, who were specialists in diplomatic precedents and procedure. Yet once they achieved supremacy, their relations with other countries were conducted from the colonial and administrative point of view, rather than from the diplomatic point of view. They did little, in fact, to create an expert body of trained negotiators.

It was during the later stages of the Roman Empire that the necessity for the art of negotiation, or of diplomacy proper, made itself felt. The Byzantine Emperors exercised this art with consummate ingenuity. They devised three main methods. The first was to weaken the barbarians by fomenting rivalry between them. The second was to purchase the friendship of frontier tribes and peoples by subsidies and flattery. And the third method was to convert the heathen to the Christian faith. It was by the concurrent employment of these three methods that Justinian was able to extend his influence over the Sudan, Arabia and Abyssinia and to keep at bay the tribes of the Black Sea and the Caucasus. Similar methods were adopted at a later stage of Byzantine history when the menace came from the Bulgarians, the Magyars and the Russians.

The constant efforts of the later Emperors to supplement their waning physical strength by diplomatic arrangements, and the particular methods which they adopted, introduced a new element into the practice of diplomacy. The method of playing off neighbouring despots one against the other rendered it essential that the Government at Constantinople should be fully informed of the ambitions, weaknesses and resources of those with whom they hoped to deal. It thus arose that the envoys of the Byzantine Emperors were instructed, not merely to represent the interests of the Empire at the courts of these barbaric despots, but also to furnish full reports as to the internal situation in foreign countries and the relation of those countries towards each other. For such purposes, qualities other than those of the herald or the orator were needed. What was required were men of trained powers of observation, long experience and sound judgment. It was in this manner that the type or character of the professional diplomatist gradually evolved. Even as the orator type replaced the primitive herald type, so also did the orator give way to the trained observer.

VI

This evolution was a slow process. It was not until the fifteenth century, when the Italian States began to appoint permanent Ambassadors, that diplomacy as a profession can be said to have been generally recognized. And even then it was not till after 1815 that the status and rules of this profession were established by international agreement.

Meanwhile, however—and concurrently with this evolution from the herald to the orator and the orator to the professional diplomatist—a further factor had gradually emerged. This factor was connected in a curious way with the origin of the word " diplomacy " itself.

That word is derived from the Greek verb " diploun " meaning " to fold." In the days of the Roman Empire all passports, passes along imperial roads and way-bills were stamped on double metal plates, folded and sewn together in a particular manner. These metal passes were called " diplomas." At a later date this word " diploma " was extended to cover other and less metallic official documents, especially those conferring privileges or embodying arrangements with foreign communities or tribes. As these treaties accumulated, the imperial archives became encumbered with innumerable little documents folded and endorsed in a particular manner. It was found necessary to employ trained clerks to index, decipher and preserve these documents. Hence the profession of archivist arose, and with it the science of palæography—the science, that is, of verifying and deciphering ancient documents. These two occupations were, until late in the seventeenth century, called "*res diplomatica*" or "diplomatic business," namely the business of dealing with archives or diplomas.

We do not always realize the importance acquired during the Middle Ages by the collection and the orderly arrangement of archives. It is no exaggeration to say that it was in the Papal and other chanceries, under the direction and authority of successive "masters of the rolls," that the usages of diplomacy as a science based upon precedent and experience first came to be established. The Carolingian chancery was elaborately organized with a full clerical staff and was placed under the charge of an official known as the "chancellor." This title (which in later Austrian and German history became of such resounding importance) derives from the name of "*cancellarius*" applied in Roman times to the man who was door-keeper at the Law Courts. Yet, in Carolingian times, no royal edict was regarded as legal unless it bore the counter-signature of the chancellor or keeper of the royal archives. It was this system which William the Conqueror established in England.

It should be remembered that the use of the terms " diplomacy " or " diplomatic " as applying, not to the study of archives, but to the conduct or management of international relations is comparatively recent. In England, it was not employed in this sense until 1796, when it was so used by Edmund Burke. And it was, as I have said above, only after the Congress of Vienna in 1815 that the diplomatic service was recognized as a profession distinct from that of the statesman or politician, or that it acquired, in definite form, its own rules, conventions and prescriptions.

The expression " diplomacy " was thus for many years associated in men's minds with the preservation of archives, the analysis of past treaties and the study of the history of international negotiations. This scientific, this scholarly, element is still vital to the functioning of any efficient Foreign Service. The British Foreign Office, for instance, possesses in its Treaty Department a body of specialists upon diplomatic procedure, in its Library a highly competent staff of experts in precedent, and in its Legal Advisers a group of technicians steeped in the niceties of treaty-drafting and international law. Without such a staff of historical and legal experts precedents would be overlooked and inaccuracies might be committed. It is thus important to emphasize what might be called the scholarly or technical origins of diplomatic practice.

The herald conception of the diplomatist waned with the realization that what was needed was something more than a stentorian voice; the orator conception waned when it was realized that it was not sufficient to send a gifted advocate but that the services of a trained observer of foreign conditions were essential to the correct estimation of policy. Yet, in spite of the Byzantine experiment, it was only gradually that the diplomatist, the legate or the "orator" (as he was for long called) came to be permanent features in international relations.

In the dark ages, and especially in feudal Europe, there was little opportunity for any orderly or established system of international contacts. Modern diplomacy as we understand it (meaning by that not only the art of negotiation but the technicians by whom that art is practised) arose during the thirteenth and fourteenth centuries in Italy. It may have been regrettable that Italy should have become the mother of organized or professional diplomacy; but it was also inevitable. The Italian city states stood outside the main feudal system; they were interconnected by countless common interests as well as sundered by ferocious rivalries ; they were constantly engaged in a competition for power and preoccupied by those combinations and alliances which might render that power predominant. It was thus in Italy during the thirteenth and fourteenth centuries that the diplomatist-statesman arose.

Florence could boast of such Ambassadors as Dante, Petrarch and Boccaccio or, at a later stage, of Machiavelli and Guicciardini. It is none the less difficult to define with exactitude when and where the vital step was taken between the temporary mission and the permanent Embassy or Legation. Scholars have identified the first experiment in permanent representation with the legatine system of the Holy See. No convincing proof can be adduced for such an origin. The first recorded permanent mission is that established at Genoa in 1455 by Francesco Sforza, Duke of Milan. Five years later the Duke of Savoy sent Eusebio Margaria, archdeacon of Vercelli, to be his permanent representative in Rome. In 1496 Venice appointed two merchants then resident in London as "*sub-ambasciatores*" on the ground that "the way to the British Isles is very long and very dangerous." And a few years later permanent Embassies of the Italian States were established in London, Paris and at the Court of Charles V. Other powers imitated this example. In 1519 Sir Thomas Boleyn and Dr. West were sent to Paris as permanent

British Ambassadors. And eventually Francis I of France devised something like a permanent diplomatic machinery.

Three centuries elapsed, however, before any diplomatic hierarchy was definitely established or recognized. In the Middle Ages diplomatic representatives were called by all manner of different names—legates, orators, nuncios, commisars, procurators, agents or ambassadors. Gradually two distinct classes came to be recognized. There was the ambassador who then, as now, was in theory the personal representative of the head of his own state. This representative quality led to endless complications. He was supposed to represent in his own person the status and dignity of his sovereign. This entailed an acute preoccupation with precedence and many unseemly wrangles, pushings and proddings in royal anterooms. Even to-day the representatives of certain minor powers are acutely sensitive to the place which they are accorded at social functions and are apt, in extreme cases of displacement (such as frequently occur in London), to feel affronted. Yet the wretched Ambassadors of the sixteenth and seventeenth centuries were not merely supposed to engage in physical combat for the maintenance of their own precedence. They were expected to indicate by the lavishness of their display the magnitude and power of their own sovereigns, and

CHAPTER II

THE DEVELOPMENT OF DIPLOMATIC THEORY

Professor Mowat's three stages—These throw too little emphasis upon the continuity of diplomatic theory—The influence of International Law—Definition of what is meant by "progress" in diplomatic theory—The Greek contribution to that progress—Arbitration and the Amphictyonic Councils—Reasons for their failure—The Roman contribution mainly legal and colonial—The Byzantine and resultant Italian theories as a reaction against the development of sound diplomatic theory—Effect of this—Sir Henry Wotton and Machiavelli—Is "moral" diplomacy inseparable from overwhelming physical power?—The influence of common sense—This arose from commercial contacts—The danger of estimating diplomatic theory solely from the ethical point of view—The immense influence of trade and commerce upon the art of negotiation—The feudal or warrior conception as contrasted with the bourgeois or shop-keeper conception—The dangers and illusions to which each of these conceptions is subject—Nature of the difference between them.

PROFESSOR MOWAT, in his valuable book, *Diplomacy and Peace*, distinguishes three periods in the development of diplomatic theory in Europe. The first of his periods runs from 476 to 1475 and covers the dark ages when diplomacy was wholly disorganized. The second period runs from 1473 to 1914 and represents that phase in history when diplomatic theory followed the system of policy known as the "European States system." The third period is that which was inaugurated by President Wilson, and from which what is sometimes known as "democratic diplomacy" has arisen.

Professor Mowat's work was published in 1935—that is before the League of Nations had fallen into discredit and before the full efficacy of anti-democratic diplomacy had become apparent. It may be doubted whether, in this year 1938, the Professor would feel so optimistic regarding his third category. It might now appear that the new gospel preached by President Wilson was neither so new nor so powerful as was at one time believed. The Wilson doctrine may be regarded by subsequent generations, not as the opening words of a new chapter in diplomatic theory, but as a footnote to the nineteenth-century conflict between the conception of a community of human interests and the conception of exclusive national rights.

In examining the emergence and development of diplomatic theory (by which I mean a generally accepted idea of the principles and methods of international conduct and negotiation) I shall avoid dividing my subject into distinct phases or categories and shall concentrate upon the continuity of this development rather than upon the sudden spurts and long retardations by which it has been marked.

It is necessary at the outset to warn the reader that the main factor in the development of diplomatic theory lies, for the most part, outside the general theme of my argument. I refer to the steady progress throughout the centuries of the conceptions and influence of what used to be called the "Law of Nations" and of what we now call (with some inexactitude) "International Law." The publication in 1625 of Grotius' *De iure belli ac pacis* ("On the law of war and peace") turned the attention of all thinking men to the problem whether there were not certain principles common to all mankind, the aggregate of which formed an actual "code" of international behaviour. Jurists have argued for centuries whether in the absence of any tribunal capable of enforcing this code, the word "Law" is exactly applicable to what are no more than suggestions of desirable principle. Yet the truth remains that the interest manifested in the "Law of Nations"; the fact that its rules and precepts were continuously being discussed and codified; and the voluntary obedience paid to its maxims by Great Powers over long stretches of time, did exert an ever-increasing influence upon the general conception of international morality, and thereby upon diplomatic theory.

The subject of International Law is, however, a lifelong study in itself. In a monograph of this nature I could only hope to touch the fringe of the matter, and since that fringe would certainly become entangled with my examination of the less juridical aspects of diplomacy, I prefer to lay it on one side. In so doing, however, I must again warn the reader that I am discarding one of the main constructive elements in the subject which I am discussing.

If, therefore, one concentrates upon the continuity of diplomatic theory rather than upon its discontinuity, one is impressed by the fact that, in spite of the several different shapes which it assumed, and in spite of dramatic periods when violence momentarily became more authoritative than reason, it is possible to recognize a distinct upward curve of progress. What is the nature of that progress? I should define it as follows: "The progress of diplomatic theory has been from the narrow conception of exclusive tribal rights to the wider conception of inclusive common interests."

It will be said that in postulating this definition I am violating my own principle of not confusing "policy" with "negotiation"; and that the progress thus defined has been a progress in policy and not a progress in the means by which policy is executed. I deny such a contention. The theory of policy and the theory of negotiation are interactive; it is not always true that the end determines the means; and all students of diplomacy will agree that diplomatists have often progressed further than politicians in their conception of international conduct, and that the servant has more than once exercised a determinant and beneficial influence upon his master.

II

In the previous chapter it was suggested that diplomatic practice gradually emerged from the herald or " white-flag " stage, to the orator or " law-court " stage. It was shown that by the fifth century the Greeks had organized something approaching a regular system of inter-state communication. Their progress in diplomatic theory was equally striking.

It is often supposed that the Greeks took as their model of the successful diplomatist, not only the titular God Hermes, but also the heroic figure of Ulysses, " fertile in expedients." Much as they admired astuteness, they admired intelligence even more. At the very same Sparta Conference which was cited in the previous chapter, a speech was delivered by King Archidamus which is almost topical in its realism :

" I have not, Lacedaemonians, reached the age that I have, without having gained experience of many wars. There are some among you of the same age as myself, who will not make the unfortunate mistake of imagining in their ignorance that war is a desirable thing or that it brings with it either advantage or security. . . .

Not that I should urge you to display so little right feeling as to allow Athens to inflict damage upon your allies. Nor should I hesitate to unmask her intrigues. But I do urge you not to rush into hostilities at once, but first to send to Athens some ambassador who would remonstrate with them in a tone, neither too suggestive of war, nor too suggestive of submission. In the meanwhile we can employ the time gained in perfecting our preparations. . . .

If the Athenians respond to our overtures, then so much the better. If they reject them, then after the lapse of two or three years our position will be much stronger and we can attack them if we think proper. It is possible even that when they realize the extent of our rearmament, backed as it will be by equally forceful representations, they will be disposed to give way. . . .

Nor should we, in a single day's debate of this kind, come to a decision which may involve the lives and fortunes of our countrymen and in which our national honour is deeply involved. We must make our decision after calm deliberation. . . . Nor should we forget that the Athenians have offered, in this Potidea crisis, to give us legal satisfaction. It is against the law to treat as a criminal a country which is prepared to offer arbitration."

The realism of King Archidamus' speech may appear to us to-day as cynical, or at least as embarrassingly outspoken. Yet his final reference to arbitration strikes a different note. How came it that a Spartan statesman, addressing a popular assembly 2,260 years before President Wilson, can have referred (at a moment of acute tension) to the method of arbitration as one which was known to, and ought to be accepted by, his audience? The fact was that the Greeks, for all the passion of their rivalries, had emerged from the theory of tribal rights to a conception of common interests. The collapse of Greek independence was due to the fact that the latter conception was not strong enough to quench the fires of the old tribal theory. But the conception existed; and in the Amphictyonic Councils it expressed itself in periodic reunions which were something between a Church Congress, an Eisteddfod and a meeting of the League of Nations Assembly.

In the seventh century the most influential of these Amphictyonic or "regional" conferences was held in the Island of Delos. When that sanctuary was despoiled by Athens the prestige of the Delian Amphictyony was transferred to Delphi. Although the main purpose of these conferences, as of the permanent secretariat which they maintained, was the safeguarding of shrines and treasures and the regulation of the pilgrim traffic, they also dealt with political matters of common Hellenic interest and, as such, had an important diplomatic function, and introduced an important diplomatic innovation.

They claimed for themselves what would now be called " exterritorial " or " diplomatic " privileges. The several States who were members of the league, or council, undertook never to destroy the city of any fellow-member and never to cut off its water supply either in war or peace. Should any member violate this article of their covenant he would automatically become an enemy of all other members who pledged themselves to go to war against him. And in fact there are many recorded instances of the Amphictyonic Councils imposing sanctions upon breakers of their covenant.

These admirable institutions failed in the end owing to two main reasons. In the first place they were never universal and many important States remained outside. In the second place they did not possess sufficient corporate force to enable them to impose their rulings upon the stronger powers. Yet their very existence served as a stabilizing influence in Greece and did much to further the conceptions of common international interests and a common international law.

III

Having reached this first high-water mark, diplomatic theory thereafter receded. The Greek City States were unable to live up to the standards of that comity of nations which they had themselves invented. Power triumphed. Alexander the Great did not possess either the Amphictyonic or the league spirit. Co-operation gave way to subordination. Liberties were lost.

The Romans, when they came, contributed the conception of international order and discipline rather than the conception of international equality or co-operation. Their contribution to diplomatic theory was of course immense; for the advantages of nimbleness and ruse, they substituted the advantages of obedience, organization, "the habit of peace," and the hatred of lawlessness. Even those who most dislike the physical gravity of the Roman system must admit that it enhanced the corporate conscience of mankind. The small, bellicose and arrogant rivalries of the tribe or clan were widened into what was in fact a world-conception. The Romans rendered not only law, but also diplomatic theory universal or œcumenical. Yet the essential benefit which they conferred (apart from the "pax romana" or world-authority) was a legal benefit. And to that extent it does not come within the scope of a study of non-juridical diplomacy.

When, in the later empire, power-policy declined, there came under the Byzantine system a recrudescence of diplomacy in its most unconstructive form. Diplomacy became the stimulant rather than the antidote to the greed and folly of mankind. Instead of co-operation, you had disintegration; instead of unity, disruption; instead of reason, you had astuteness; in the place of moral principles you had ingenuity. The Byzantine conception of diplomacy was directly transmitted to Venice, and, from those fœtid lagoons, throughout the Italian peninsula. Diplomacy in the Middle Ages had a predominately Italian, and indeed Byzantine, flavour. It is to this heredity that it owes, in modern Europe, so much of its disrepute.

It is interesting to consider how it came that diplomacy, which in its essence is common sense and charity applied to international relations, should have acquired such a dubious reputation. It is perhaps not too invidious or far-fetched to explain this unhappy prejudice by the fact that it reached feudal Europe from Byzantium via the Italian city states.

Admittedly, the standards of European diplomacy, when it first asserted itself as a distinctive calling, were not high standards. The diplomatists of the sixteenth and seventeenth centuries often provided ground for the suspicion from which their successors have unjustifiably suffered. They bribed courtiers; they stimulated and financed rebellions; they encouraged opposition parties; they intervened in the most subversive ways in the internal affairs of the countries to which they were accredited; they lied, they spied, they stole.

An ambassador in those days regarded himself as "an honourable spy." He was sincerely convinced that private morality was a thing apart from public morality. Many of them imagined that "the official lie" bore but slight relation to individual mendacity. Nor did they for one moment realize that it was not merely unbecoming, but actually ineffective, for a man of honour and integrity to mislead foreign Governments by deliberate distortions of fact.

It was a British Ambassador, Sir Henry Wotton, who expressed the view that "an ambassador is an honest man who is sent to lie abroad for the good of his country." That phrase is often quoted against us. What is not stated is, that Sir Henry scribbled this remark as a joke in an album at Augsburg. The remark was discovered by one of his enemies, who reported it to James I. That monarch was profoundly shocked by the cynicism of his envoy; in vain did Wotton plead that he had scribbled this apophthegm merely as a "merriment." King James refused to employ him again.

The ill repute enjoyed by diplomatists among the general public was not due only to such chance jests as that of Sir Henry Wotton. More importantly, it can be ascribed to the progressive identification of the theory and practice of diplomacy with the precepts of Machiavelli. It is a curious fact that although *The Prince* of Niccolò Machiavelli was written in 1513, an English translation was only issued in 1640. Meanwhile, a garbled version of his ideas had percolated into Great Britain and had created the word " machiavellian." As early as 1579 and 1592 we find Stubbes and Nashe using the adjective " macciavelian " and the substantive " machiavilisme."

Machiavelli's main intention was to warn his age against the dangers of weak government:

" You must know," he writes, " that there are two methods of fighting, the one by law, the other by force; the first method is that of men, the second of beasts; but as the first method is often insufficient, one must have recourse to the second."

This, considering the date at which it was written, may appear realistic, but it is not cynical. It was the distortion, rather than the text, of Machiavelli's theory which caused the damage and created the epithet. And it must be admitted that there are passages in *The Prince* which gave grounds for the false impression induced.

" How laudable," he writes, " it is for a prince to keep good faith and live with integrity, and not with astuteness, everyone knows. Still the experience of our time shows those princes to have done great things who have had little regard for good faith, and have been able by astuteness to confuse men's brains and have ultimately overcome those who have made loyalty their foundation. . . . Therefore a prudent ruler ought not to keep faith when by so doing it would be against his interest, and when the reasons which made him bind himself no longer exist. If men were all good, this precept would not be a good one ; but as they are bad, and would not observe faith with you, so you are not bound to keep faith with them."

Phrases such as these, which in fact occur but rarely in Machiavelli's memorable writings, were widely quoted at the time ; and the public derived therefrom an incorrect impression that such principles, rather than honesty and good sense, were in fact at the root of all international negotiation and were those which any aspiring diplomatist was bound to observe.

IV

I have sketched the development of diplomatic theory from primitive times to the point where, towards the middle of the sixteenth century, it begins to assume a modern tinge. I have shown how the Greeks endeavoured, but failed, to establish the conception of a community of nations, the joint interests of which were more important and more valuable than the sectional interests of individual States. I have shown how the Romans introduced the conception of international law, and how they were able by the very magnitude of their Empire to impose the memory of a universal State. In later centuries the Church of Rome and the Holy Roman Empire endeavoured, although with diminishing success, to perpetuate this memory. I have indicated how, with the decline of imperial preponderance, diplomatic theory became Byzantine; and how Constantinople bequeathed to the Italian States the theory that diplomacy was the ally rather than the enemy of force and lawlessness.

The observant cynic might contend that the course of this development proves that diplomacy only becomes moral when it is the servant of overwhelming power, or that nations only subordinate to the common weal their individual interests and ambitions when they are faced by a menace which threatens all. There is some truth in this contention. The Greeks succeeded in their experiment when they were threatened by Persia and relapsed into internecine conflict when the danger had passed. The high ideals of their Amphictyons failed because there was not one of their members sufficiently powerful to impose unselfishness upon the others. The Romans again were only able to establish the rule of international law and the "habit of peace" when they had become unquestioned masters of the known world. Similarly, once that mastery declined, diplomatic theory degenerated from its world conception and became, under the Byzantines and the Italians, predatory, disruptive and mean.

Yet if we consider the continuity of diplomatic theory and examine the graph of its development, we shall find that this graph (although at every stage of the world's history there have been moments, as now, when it becomes seismographic) does show an ascending line. What were the influences that made for this improvement?

The first was law; the second was commerce. It is the latter influence which I shall now consider.

Anglo-Saxon writers on diplomatic theory display a tendency to attribute such improvements as they can record in the standards of that theory to the spread of moral enlightenment. They contend that the advance of diplomatic theory is to be measured, not only by the increase in the conception of a community of human interests, but also by the gradual approximation of public to private morality.

Such approximation is unquestionably an ideal towards which all good diplomatists should strive. Yet there has always existed, and there still exists, a school of continental theorists who contend that the safety and interests of one's own State constitute the supreme moral law; and that it is merely sentimental to contend that the ethical conventions which govern the relations of individuals between themselves have ever, or should ever, be applied to the relations between sovereign States. One is tempted, of course, to dismiss such a theory as ignoble and reactionary and to contrast it with the shining purity of its opposite. Yet in fact the doctrine of "My country right or wrong" makes a powerful appeal to many millions of quite civilized people; it can even stimulate such virtues as self-sacrifice, discipline and energy; and it provides diplomacy with directives which are at once more potent and more precise than the vague aspirations of the enlightened.

My own practical experience, and the years of study which I have devoted to this subject, have left me with the profound conviction that "moral" diplomacy is ultimately the most effective, and that "immoral" diplomacy defeats its own purposes. Yet I should hesitate, in commenting upon the art of negotiation, to attribute its development solely to ethical impulses. These impulses have done much to foster a sounder diplomatic theory, and they are operative even to-day. Yet to exaggerate their influence would be to distort the actual proportions of development, might lead one to regard one school of thought as "good" and the other school as "bad," and might thereby expose one to the terrible dangers of selfrighteousness, partisanship, or even moral indignation.

Diplomacy is not a system of moral philosophy; it is, as Sir Ernest Satow defined it, "the application of intelligence and tact to the conduct of official relations between the governments of independent States." The worst kind of diplomatists are missionaries, fanatics and lawyers; the best kind are the reasonable and humane sceptics. Thus it is not religion which has been the main formative influence in diplomatic theory; it is common sense. And it was through trade and commerce that people first learnt to apply common sense in their dealings with each other.

It is beyond the scope of this monograph to examine the stages by which international trade emerged from the chaos of the dark ages and the feudal system into the calmer waters of the Middle Ages. I do not propose to discuss the influence upon commerce of the Crusades, of the Venetian monopoly, or of the fall of the Eastern Empire. A few dates will suffice. The Hanseatic League was founded as early as 1241. The Canary Islands were first sighted in 1330. Vasco da Gama reached India by the Cape in 1497. The Portuguese founded Macao in 1537. The Italian City States established consuls in the Levant as early as 1196.

It was in this manner that the theory of diplomacy developed upon several parallel lines. There was Roman law and the memory of a world-state capable of rendering it international. There was the Byzantine tradition of ingenuity. There was the imperial legacy of power-politics, leading to the conception of diplomacy as an adjunct to the military feudal caste. There was the papal idea of a world discipline resting upon religious sanctions. And in and out of these glittering strands of development, ran the homely worsted of the mercantile conception of a diplomacy governed by the reasonable bargaining of man with man. Sound diplomacy was the invention of middle-class citizens.

V

In the centuries that followed (and apart from technical differences in aim and procedure which will be noted in the following chapter) two main currents of diplomatic theory can be differentiated. The first was the theory of the military and political caste which survived the feudal system. The second was a more bourgeois conception which arose from the contacts of commerce. The former tended towards power-politics and was much concerned with such associations as national prestige, status, precedence, and glamour. The latter tended towards profit-politics, and was mainly preoccupied with appeasement, conciliation, compromise, and credit. True it is that these tendencies frequently overlapped. There were periods during which the feudal conception became extremely pacifist; there were times when the bourgeois conception became violently provocative. Yet, on the whole, it is the difference between these two tendencies, the feudal tendency and the bourgeois tendency, which throw a clearer light upon the development and present condition of diplomacy than any search for abstruse and inapplicable moral conceptions.

Let us call the first "the warrior or heroic" theory; and the second the "mercantile or shopkeeper" theory. The former regards diplomacy as "war by other means": the latter regards it as an aid to peaceful commerce.

It is not only the aims of the warrior school which are predatory. The methods by which they give effect to those policies are conceived and managed from the military rather than from the civilian point of view. Negotiation under such a system resembles a military campaign, or, at the best, autumn manœuvres; and the means which such negotiators employ are more akin to military tactics than to the give and take of civilian intercourse.

Fundamental to such a conception of diplomacy is the belief that the purpose of negotiation is victory, and that the denial of complete victory means defeat. Diplomacy is regarded as an unremitting activity directed towards ultimate triumph. The strategy of negotiation thus becomes an endeavour to out-flank your opponent, to occupy strategical positions which are at once consolidated before any further advance is made; to weaken the enemy by all manner of attacks behind the lines; to seek for every occasion to drive a wedge between your main enemy and his allies; and to hold your opponents on one position while planning an attack elsewhere. The actual tactics employed by these negotiators are also military in character. You have the surprise, and often the night, attack; you have the trench-raid or "*Kraftprobe*" designed to test the strength of the enemy's position at any given point; you have the strategical retreat at moments, and the stealthy occupation of key positions; you have intimidation, ruthlessness and force; and you have elaborate containing actions while your main forces are being massed in some other direction.

It is obvious that under such a system conciliation, confidence and fair-dealing are not very apparent. A concession made, a treaty concluded, is apt to be regarded, not as the final settlement of an isolated dispute, but as evidences of weakness and retreat, as an advantage which must immediately be exploited in preparation for further triumphs.

As opposed to this warrior conception of diplomacy, there stands the commercial, the mercantile or the shop-keeper conception. This civilian theory of negotiation is based upon the assumption that a compromise between rivalries is generally more profitable than the complete destruction of the rival. That negotiation is not a mere phase in a death-struggle, but an attempt by mutual concession to reach some durable understanding. That "national honour" must be interpreted as "national honesty" and that questions of prestige should not be allowed to interfere unduly with a sound business deal. That there is probably some middle point between the two negotiators which, if discovered, should reconcile their conflicting interests. And that to find this middle point, all that is required is a frank discussion, the placing of cards upon the table, and the usual processes of human reason, confidence and fair-dealing.

Each of these two theories has its peculiar dangers as its peculiar illusions. Yet the greatest danger of all is the inability of the military school to understand the sincerity of the civilian school and the failure of the shop-keepers to realize that the warriors are inspired by a totally different idea of the means and purposes of negotiation. The former believe far too much in the ability of force to produce intimidation; the latter believe far too much in the ability of the credit idea to produce confidence. The latter wish to inspire confidence, the former hope to create fear. This difference in conception creates, on the one side resentment, and on the other contemptuous suspicion.

From the emphasis which I have laid upon these two divergent tendencies, it will have been observed that I believe that the development of diplomatic theory has been (and still is) more dependent upon the contrast between imagination and reason, between the romantic and the sensible, between the heroic and the mercantile, than upon any ascertainable standards of moral values. In each of the two tendencies there exists both idealism and realism. What really separates them is that the former is essentially a dynamic theory whereas the latter is static. The one needs movement for its expression, the other requires calm.

CHAPTER III

THE TRANSITION FROM THE OLD DIPLOMACY TO THE NEW

Is there any difference between "old" and "new" diplomacy ?—Views of Jules Cambon—Illustration from Soviet Diplomacy—A transition rather than a contrast —Diplomacy as reflecting changes in systems of government—Diplomacy under monarchic absolutism—Boudoir diplomacy—Catherine II and Malmesbury as an instance of this—The rise of constitutional monarchy—The International of the Monarchs—William II and the Tsar—The Björkoe Treaty—Edward VII—Queen Victoria—The essential fact that a negotiator must represent the sovereign authority in his own country—President Wilson not sufficiently representative—From autocracy to democracy—Three main factors of development—(1) The conception of common European interests—Canning and Metternich—the "Concert of Europe"—(2) The belief in the force of public opinion—Canning and Palmerston—(3) Improvement in communications —The effect of the telephone upon diplomatic practice —The essential importance in an Ambassador of personal character—The old diplomatist—The freemasonry of professional diplomacy—Value of such freemasonry

All really good people speak of the "Old Diplomacy,"—as also of her disreputable friend "Secret Diplomacy,"—in a tone of moral censure. The implication is that, somewhere about the year 1918, diplomacy saw a great white light, was converted, found salvation, and thereafter and thenceforward became an entirely different woman.

Marked differences do in fact exist between the diplomacy of the seventeenth or eighteenth centuries and the diplomacy of to-day. It would be a mistake, however, to examine these differences as if they were sharp contrasts between *their* darkness and *our* light. No sudden conversion has taken place; no sharp contrasts of principle or method can be recognized; all that has happened is that the art of negotiation has gradually adjusted itself to changes in political conditions.

Monsieur Jules Cambon (himself one of the most intelligent and high-minded of professional diplomatists) has gone so far as to contend that the alleged difference between the old and the new diplomacy is a popular illusion:

"To talk," he writes, "about new and old diplomacy is to make a distinction without a difference. It is the outward appearance, or, if you like, the make-up of diplomacy which is gradually changing. The substance will remain—firstly because human nature never changes; secondly because there is only one way of settling international differences; and lastly because the most persuasive method at the disposal of a government is the word of an honest man."

It is true that diplomacy is a continuous process and that its basic principles represent the accumulated experience of generations of wise and reasonable men. It is also true that those who deride the rules and formulas of diplomacy are apt to find in practice that these prescriptions are not so vain or so empty as was at first supposed. Had M. Cambon so desired, he might have illustrated his point by an examination of Soviet diplomatic methods since 1917. These methods were at first proclaimed with all the apparatus of a new revelation. The speeches which the Soviet representatives delivered at the Conference of Brest-Litovsk were published as and when they were delivered. Immense perplexity, tribulation and boredom were thereby occasioned to the patient millions of the U.S.S.R.; nor, when one considers the final terms of that *diktat*, was this open covenant any the better for having been so openly arrived at. The rank and title of "Ambassador" was expunged from the Soviet vocabulary and for a space of time the accredited representatives of the U.S.S.R. were called by the ungainly name of "Polpreds." And the manner adopted by these missionaries of a new system combined, at first, the sturdy ruggedness of a triumphant proletariat with that other-world smile of conscious moral superiority which one associates with all recent converts to a new religion.

As the years passed, however, the U.S.S.R.

relapsed not ungracefully into the manner of the older convention. Their polpreds in Iran and China were suddenly nominated ambassadors, since it was by this means only that the Soviet embassy could acquire precedence over the legations of the other powers. The negotiations which led up to the Treaty of Rapallo were conducted in the secrecy of a hotel bedroom, and the ensuing treaty burst like a bombshell upon a startled world. And with the waning of their first fine careless rapture, the style, the behaviour, the external appearance and the urbanity of the representatives of Soviet Russia approximated ever close and closer to that of pre-war Balkan diplomatists.

Yet in spite of M. Cambon's contention, and in spite of many other illustrations which might be adduced to support it, the fact remains that the development of diplomatic practice and theory is marked by certain transitions. In the present chapter I propose to examine by what stages the Old Diplomacy merged into the New.

II

It would be agreeable, but inaccurate, to contend that the line of advance from the old to the new diplomacy has been one from absolutism, via a governing class, to democratic control. True it is that in Great Britain the adjustments of diplomacy to policy have in fact followed some such line.

But this would not be true of other countries. Herr Hitler, for instance, is far more absolutist than were either William II or Bismarck; Signor Mussolini is far more autocratic than were Crispi or Cavour. Diplomacy during the last twenty years has become more personal, more secret, more occult even, than it was in the later nineteenth century. So far from having died in 1918, the old diplomacy is to-day more dynamic and more assertive than the new.

It is possible, of course, to dismiss this inconvenient fact as a temporary reversion to an outworn and discredited theory. That may be true. Yet it is simpler and more precise to contend that a certain political system inevitably reflects itself in a certain type of diplomatic practice and theory. Such changes as occur are due, less to any alternation in ethical standards, than to a shift in the centre of power. In examining transitions from the old diplomacy I shall emphasize and explain this contention.

In the days of absolute monarchy a country, together with its inhabitants, was regarded as the absolute property of the reigning sovereign. Thus Louis XIV and, to an even greater extent, Catherine II and Frederick the Great, retained the conduct of foreign policy, the issues of peace or war, within their own hands. They were the "sovereign authority," not in name only, but also in fact. Inevitably under such a system diplomacy and policy became inextricably mixed; negotiation became an intimate problem of personalities; and it was highly important that an Ambassador should secure the confidence, and if possible the affections, of the sovereign to whom he was accredited.

This necessity led to many shabby expedients. Not only did diplomatists in those days pay large bribes to court functionaries, not only did they wrangle interminably over precedence and status, not only did they steal official documents, but they strove by every means in their power to win the support of the reigning favourite or, if that were impossible, to secure his or her replacement by some successor more amenable to their influence.

An admirable instance of this "boudoir diplomacy" is afforded by the mission of Sir James Harris (Lord Malmesbury) to St. Petersburg in 1779. That Harris was regarded as one of the most skilled exponents of eighteenth-century diplomacy is made clear by the eulogy of Talleyrand. "I hold him," he said, "to have been the ablest Minister of his time—it was impossible to surpass him, all one could do was to follow him as closely as possible." Yet the fact remains that neither in Russia nor in Holland did Harris achieve very much.

His methods in St. Petersburg were typical of

the period. The aim of his mission was to induce the Empress Catherine to ally herself with Great Britain. The Empress flirted with the idea even as she flirted with the Ambassador. Harris's reports give a vivid picture of the general atmosphere of boudoir diplomacy:

"On Monday," he writes, "at the masquerade given at the Grand-Duchess' birthday, some time after her Imperial Majesty's card-party, at which I had assisted, was finished, M. Korsakoff came up to me, and desiring me to follow him, conducted me a back way into the Empress' private dressing-room, and on introducing me, immediately retired. The Empress, after making me sit down, began by saying that after her own affairs, ours were those which she had most at heart and she would be happy if I could obviate the obstacles which ever presented themselves to her mind in every plan she had formed to be useful to us."

Thus encouraged, the Ambassador suggested that the Empress might make a naval demonstration against France and Spain. The Empress remarked that surely the British fleet was a match for those of our enemies, and that if we really wanted peace we should give the American Colonies their freedom. Harris asked her whether if she were Queen of England she would make any such sacrifice. She replied that she would rather have her head cut off. She then pointed out, with justice, that this was no Russian quarrel and that she saw no reason why she should risk the Russian fleet in western waters. Harris pointed out to her that she would acquire much honour and glory by such an escapade. "She seemed," he records, "much pleased with the idea." Yet she evaded committing herself. "Our conversation," Sir James adds, "having lasted upwards of an hour, she dismissed me, and it being quite dark it was with some difficulty I found my way through the intricate passages back to the ballroom."

Harris did not relax his efforts. He became intimate with Potemkin. He gave large sums of money to the favourite's friends. He did everything within his power to destroy the influence of Catherine's chief minister, Panin. Nor did he fail to press his suit upon the Empress. "Were I a younger woman," she said to him, "I might be less prudent." Harris was a fine-looking man and the Empress was susceptible; this was personal diplomacy at its most intoxicating, yet in the end Harris returned to London having achieved but little and being the poorer in his own pocket by over £20,000.

III

The memoirs of James Harris, Earl of Malmesbury, do in fact show us monarchical diplomacy at its very worst. His subsequent transactions in Holland were, by our present standards, equally deplorable. Yet it must be remembered that a diplomatist is bound to take conditions in foreign countries as he finds them. It is possible, and even probable, that it was irksome for Harris to be obliged to flirt with an Empress who was over fifty years of age, even as it was unpleasant for him to watch his wife being taken in to supper by Potemkin; yet the old diplomacy took a heavy toll upon personal predilections and even to-day an ambassador who allowed his dislike of foreign personalities or conditions to become apparent would not in fact be serving the purposes for which he had been appointed.

With the rise of constitutional monarchy, boudoir diplomacy began to wane. Yet throughout the nineteenth century, and in fact until 1918, the theory persisted that diplomacy was in some special sense identified with the person of the reigning monarch. The Emperor William II, for instance, was often apt to imagine that he was in some degree his own foreign minister. He minuted despatches, he made appointments, he issued instructions. His correspondence with the Emperor of Russia, which was published by the Soviet Government, is in itself evidence of the great responsibility which he assumed for the conduct of diplomacy. He went further. In

July 1905 he arranged a secret meeting with the Tsar at Björkoe in Finland. There, in the cabin of the Russian Imperial yacht, he obliged his amiable cousin to sign a personal treaty of alliance between Germany and Russia. The monarchs were overjoyed, but when each of them returned to his capital their Ministers refused to endorse the treaty. Much to the humiliation of the two Emperors, the Björkoe arrangement was declared null and void. For in the earlier years of the nineteenth century it was still considered unfitting that the whims, emotions or affections of individuals should determine the policy of their countries.

It was not only in autocratic, or semi-autocratic, countries that monarchs, until 1918, regarded themselves as standing in some special relation to diplomacy. The part played by King Edward VII in international affairs has been much exaggerated. Yet it is true that he regarded ambassadors as his personal representatives in something more than a technical sense, and it is also true that until his death he claimed to be closely consulted in regard to foreign policy. Nor were the Governments of his time at all averse from according him this special position. His experience was immense; his knowledge great; his tact unsurpassed. In his own person he was a most potent Ambassador and his state visits to foreign capitals, as well as the conversations which he held with foreign statesmen in continental watering-places, had without question an important, and on the whole a useful, effect upon negotiation. It would be a mistake, however, to suppose that King Edward VII ever acted unconstitutionally or that his diplomatic activities were undertaken without the knowledge and warm approval of his responsible ministers.

Foreign policy, moreover (and with it diplomacy), was, during the nineteenth century and during the first fourteen years of the twentieth, not unaffected by what has been called " the international of the monarchs." Inevitably these crowned heads established some sort of freemasonry between themselves; loyal though they mostly were to their constitutional positions and to their own ministers and subjects, yet they were drawn to each other, not only by a common monarchical principle, but by that very loneliness which gapes around a throne. Nor was this all. A matriarch such as Queen Victoria, a patriarch such as Christian IX of Denmark, were in fact closely related to most of the reigning houses of Europe. Queen Victoria was temperamentally domestic and her family feelings were acute and at moments forcible. She dominated her cosmopolitan family by a network of private correspondence which, although in appearance naïve and sentimental, was in fact instinct with sound common sense. There can be little doubt that her family sermons to the German

Empress and to Alexander II were effective in preventing Bismarck from declaring war against France in 1875. In all her vast correspondence there are few instances of disloyalty to her own ministers or of indiscretion. Even Mr. Gladstone, who was a not too partial witness, bears testimony to the value of her family connections :

" Personal and domestic relations with the ruling families abroad give openings, in delicate cases, for saying more, and saying it at once more gently and more efficaciously than could be ventured in the more formal correspondence and under contacts of Governments."

IV

Yet although monarchical influence lingered long in the practice and theory of diplomacy, the real centre of the machine shifted, from 1815 onwards, from the Court to the Cabinet. It was this change in the focus of power which gradually altered diplomatic methods.

It is obvious that if negotiation between one country and another is to achieve any practical result, the negotiator must represent the actual, as distinct from the theoretical, sovereign authority in his own country. This rule applies to all and every form of negotiation. Thus a representative sent by the Midland Bank to negotiate a loan with J. P. Morgan Company would have to be certain, not only that he had his own directors behind him, but that those with whom he negotiated were speaking with the full authority of 23 Wall Street.

Many of the disasters of diplomacy have been due to the fact that this fully representative quality has not been, on one side or the other, fully secured. Governments fall and are succeeded by their opponents. A negotiator, for instance, who had been despatched by a Republican administration might find that in the middle of his negotiations that administration had been succeeded by an administration of Democrats, who might, or might not, accord him the same confidence as had their predecessors. Similarly, the authorities with whom he was negotiating might in their turn be on the verge of electoral or revolutionary defeat, and might in fact be unrepresentative of the real centres of power in their own countries.

Thus the Treaty of Björkoe came to nothing since (in spite of theoretical sovereignty) the two negotiators of that agreement did not, in the last resort, represent in their persons the supreme authority in their own countries. An even more painful and embarrassing instance of incomplete representation is provided by the position of President Wilson at the Paris Peace Conference. On the one hand he was the chief executive officer of the United States and his credentials were not by any possible means open to question. On the other hand it was generally known that he was not fully representative of the central authority in his own country, namely the American electorate. A most difficult dilemma was thereby created for those who were obliged to negotiate with the President. They could not say that he did not represent the United States, since in theory he did; they did not feel that he represented the determining authority in his own country because they knew that in practice he did not. They therefore compromised between the ideals of the President and their own most urgent needs. If the treaties of peace had been wholly Wilson or wholly Clemenceau they might, in either case, have stood some chance of survival; it was the attempt to combine two opposites which rendered them neither real nor ideal; and this unfortunate combination of opposites was largely due to the fact that the President in 1919 was not fully representative of his own sovereign.

I have cited these instances not only in order to show how damaging a situation is created when the accredited representative of a country is not possessed of the moral, as well as the technical, mandate of those for whom he speaks; but for the purpose of indicating how sensitive is diplomacy or negotiation to any shifting in the incidence of sovereignty. The old diplomacy was obliged to adopt the ideas and habits of the systems which it represented. As those systems changed, diplomacy, although with a noticeable time-lag, changed with them. It is a grave error to suppose that any diplomacy could prove effective if it ceased to retain the confidence and support of the sovereign power in its own country, or to imagine that the "old diplomacy" possessed some organic existence of its own, independent of the sovereign authority from which it drew its very life-blood.

Thus when, during the course of the nineteenth century, the old theories of diplomacy appeared to be adopting new shapes, it was in fact not the diplomatists who were undergoing a change of heart but the political systems which they represented. A description of the transition between "old" and "new" diplomacy would thus entail a description of the whole democratic trends of the last hundred years. This would obviously be beyond the scope of this monograph. Yet it is possible to distinguish, among the innumerable influences which shaped modern democracies, three special factors which exercised a specific effect upon the methods and theory of international negotiation. These three factors were: first a growing sense of the community of nations; secondly an increasing appreciation of the importance of public opinion; and thirdly the rapid increase in communications.

V

I have already stated that the development of diplomatic theory in democratic States has been from the conception of exclusive national rights towards a conception of common international interests. This movement, if it is to triumph over selfish or regional prejudices, requires the impulse of a common external danger. It was fear of Persia which for a time cemented the Greek States into some form of solidarity; it was the French Revolution and the Napoleonic danger which provided a similar impulse in the nineteenth century. Historians ascribe the first conception of this common European interest to the circular of Count Kaunitz of July 17, 1791. In this circular he urged the powers to unite to "preserve public peace, the tranquility of States, the inviolability of possessions, and the faith of treaties."

True it is that after 1815, when the danger was removed, this fine conception degenerated into an alliance of the victorious powers and that, under the influence of Alexander I, it was twisted into an anti-comintern pact. True it is also that the England of Canning revolted against the Congress System, the Holy Alliance and Metternich's conception of a federation of Europe. Yet, throughout the nineteenth century, such phrases as "The General System of Europe," or "The Concert of

Europe," or, more familiarly, "The Concert," perpetuated the theory of a community of European nations. Even Mr. Gladstone, in 1879, felt obliged to place the Concert of Europe among those principles of foreign policy which he preached during the Midlothian campaign:

"In my opinion," he said, "the third sound principle is this: to strive to cultivate and maintain, ay, to the very uttermost, what is called the Concert of Europe, to keep the Powers of Europe in union together. And why? Because keeping all in union together you neutralize and fetter and bind up the selfish aims of each."

It is incorrect to dismiss the conception of the Concert of Europe as a purely inoperative diplomatic catchword or as a phrase designed to justify the domination of the Great Powers. It was more than that. It represented a tacit understanding between the five Great Powers that there were certain common standards of dignity, humanity and good faith which should govern the conduct of these Powers in their relations with each other and in their dealings with less potent or less civilized communities. When, in 1914, this whole conception was shattered, something of great stabilizing value, something of durable common repute, passed from the policies of Europe.

The second great factor in the development of

diplomatic theory during the nineteenth century was the growing realization of the importance of public opinion. To a diplomatist of the old school such as Metternich the very idea that the public should have any knowledge of, or opinion upon, foreign policy appeared both dangerous and fantastic. Canning, on the other hand, regarded public opinion as something which, so far from being avoided, should actually be invoked. It was mainly for this reason that Metternich described him as "a malevolent meteor hurled by divine providence upon Europe."

For to Canning public opinion was "a power more tremendous than was perhaps ever yet brought into action in the history of mankind." Palmerston was of the same view. "Opinions," he said, "are stronger than armies. Opinions, if they are founded in truth and justice, will in the end prevail against the bayonets of infantry, the fire of artillery and the charges of cavalry." The force of this conviction sometimes led Lord Palmerston astray. The opinion of the Danes upon the question of Schleswig-Holstein was unquestionably "founded in truth and justice," but it failed, much to Palmerston's dismay, to triumph over Bismarck's grenadiers. Moreover, Palmerston, as most British statesmen, was subject to the fallacy that foreign public opinion is akin to our own; he imagined that if public opinion on the Continent were allowed to express itself, peace would inevitably result; nor did he realize that on occasions popular emotion may, when once unleashed, be more dangerous than any diplomatic machinations.

The problem of diplomacy and public opinion is one of some complexity and will be discussed at length in the following chapter. It is sufficient to record that during the nineteenth century the regard for (and sometimes, as with Bismarck, the deliberate exploitation of) public opinion became an ever increasing factor in the transition between the old diplomacy and the new.

A third factor in this transition was the improvement in communications. The steam engine, the telegraph, the aeroplane and the telephone have done much to modify the practices of the old diplomacy. In the seventeenth and eighteenth centuries an ambassador was despatched with written instructions indicating to him the general line which he should follow and the main purposes which he should strive to achieve. Once he reached his post he became almost cut off from his own government and had to steer his course by his own compass and under alien stars. To-day an ambassador, if he is uncertain regarding the slightest detail of his action, can telephone within a few minutes to Downing Street, whereas his Foreign Secretary or even his Prime Minister is apt, at any moment, to descend upon him from the sky. It is obvious, therefore, that the qualities of personal initiative, enterprise and responsibility are less severely strained in the new diplomacy than they were in the old.

It would be an exaggeration, none the less, to contend that the modern ambassador is, in comparison to his predecessors in the eighteenth century, no more than a clerk at the end of the telephone. In the first place most of the eighteenth century envoys were so terrified of committing their governments or of having their notes and actions repudiated, that they preferred to take no action at all. We remember the sensational ambassadors of the pre-telegraph days such as Malmesbury and Elliot, Stratford Canning and Bulwer. The enterprise, the resource, and the ingenuity of these legates were in fact terrifying. But we forget the other long succession of drab envoys, too timid to take the initiative, too exiled to be very happy, too lazy even to write a report. The telegraph has at least prevented the former type from landing us in war and the latter type from hiding amicably behind their own laziness and inefficiency.

Conversely, in an age when personality is again becoming one of the decisive factors in politics, the character and intelligence of an ambassador are of vital significance. Exactly the same qualities may not be required to-day as were required in the eighteenth century. Yet to-day, as then, the policy of a Cabinet can only be rightly executed if they possess as their representative on the spot a man of experience, integrity, and intelligence; a man of resource, good-temper and courage; a man, above all, who is not swayed by emotion or prejudice, who is profoundly modest in all his dealings, who is guided only by a sense of public duty, and who understands the perils of cleverness and the virtues of reason, moderation, discretion, patience and tact. Mere telephone clerks are not, in so far as I am aware, expected to display all these difficult qualities at once.

VI

By such slow stages, through such various channels, has the great river of diplomacy changed its bed. The water is the same as formerly, the river is fed by the same tributaries and performs much the same functions. It is merely that it has shifted itself a mile or so in the sand.

It will always be desirable that the foreign policy of any great country should be carried out by professionals trained in their business. Amateur diplomatists (as the United States and the U.S.S.R. are coming to recognize) are prone to prove unreliable. It is not merely that their lack of knowledge and experience may be of disadvantage to their governments, it is that the amateur diplomatist is apt out of vanity and owing to the shortness of his tenure to seek for rapid successes; that he tends, owing to diffidence, to be over-suspicious; that he is inclined to be far too zealous and to have bright ideas; that he has not acquired the humane and tolerant disbelief which is the product of a long diplomatic career and is often assailed by convictions, sympathies, even impulses; that he may arrive with a righteous contempt for the formalities of diplomacy and with some impatience of its conventions; that he may cause offence when he wishes only to inspire geniality; and that in his reports and despatches he may seek rather to display his own acumen and literary brilliance than to provide his government with a careful and sensible balance-sheet of facts.

The old diplomatist, from the days of La Bruyère to those of Marcel Proust, has been frequently ridiculed and at times abused. He is represented sometimes as a man of infinite cunning and sometimes as a dotard of incredible ineptitude. The professional diplomatist does, it must be admitted, acquire a habit of conventional suavity which is sometimes irritating. Yet he also acquires, during the course of his experience, many estimable qualities which will be considered hereafter.

More important, perhaps, is the corporate feeling which the diplomatic service creates. Even as scientists, philatelists and other experts find, when they meet together, that the interests of their calling transcend all differences of nationality or language, so also do the diplomatic services of the several countries evolve a form of solidarity and establish certain tacit standards which they all respect. A man who has spent his life in the foreign service of his country has either met or known by reputation most of the professional diplomatists of his age. In later years an ambassador and the head of some foreign Ministry may find that they were young attachés together before the war. They thus possess an estimate of each other's reliability and intelligence which is based upon long experience rather than upon instinctive supposition. At the best, this produces absolute mutual confidence; at the worst, it provides the negotiators on each side with an accurate assessment of each other's turpitude.

Nor is this all. As in other walks of life, and as in other professions, a man is ultimately judged, not by his brilliance, but by his rectitude. The professional diplomatist, as other men, desires deeply to be regarded as a man of honour by those whom he respects. One of the advantages of professional diplomacy under the former system was that it produced and maintained a corporate estimate of character. It was the Stock Market of diplomatic reputation. It was generally known that men such as Bülow, Aerenthal and Iswolsky were not to be wholly trusted; it was generally known that upon such men as Bethmann-Hollweg, the two Cambons, and Stolypin one could rely. With the passing of professional diplomacy this expert estimation of character will also pass. Nor will the business of international negotiation profit thereby.

CHAPTER IV

DEMOCRATIC DIPLOMACY

Certain axioms show that diplomacy is the servant of the public—Had these axioms been clearly understood the confusion regarding " secret diplomacy " need not have arisen—President Wilson and his " open covenants " —The difference between his theory and his practice—Yet in fact in 1919 democratic control of foreign policy was secured—Firstly by Article 18 of the League Covenant —And secondly by the new practice of ratification—Examination of that new practice—Its merits and defects —The main dangers of democratic diplomacy—Irresponsibility of the sovereign people—Their ignorance and lethargy in regard to foreign affairs—The slowness of democratic diplomacy—Its imprecision—Effect of democratic control upon the practice of diplomacy—The publicity problem—Diplomacy and the Press—The politician as negotiator—Disadvantages of this practice —How is democratic diplomacy to discover its own formula ?

THE function of diplomacy is the management of the relations between independent States by processes of negotiation. The professional diplomatist is the servant of the sovereign authority in his own country. In democratic countries, that sovereign authority is represented, in the first place by a majority of the House of Commons, and in the second place by the Government or

Cabinet to whom that majority accords executive powers.

It may be true, as Rousseau contended, that " the sovereign people " in democratic countries only exercise their sovereignty during a general election, and that thereafter, and for a period of some four years, it is only a proportion of the sovereign people (namely the majority at the previous general election) who actually govern. It may be true also that even their governance and control is so indirect as to be merely vicarious, and that during the lifetime of any given Parliament or Administration, the majority may have shifted from one side to the other. To that extent representative government is based upon a fiction ; yet it must be admitted that on the whole it is the fairest and most convenient fiction that the brain of man has yet been able to devise.

The civil service, of which the diplomatic service is a branch, is supposed to possess no politics. Its duty is to place its experience at the disposal of the Government in power, to tender advice, and if need be to raise objections. Yet, if that advice be disregarded by the Minister, as representative of the sovereign people, it is the duty and function of the civil service to execute his instructions without further question.

There is an implicit contract, under this system. between the Government and the civil service,

The latter are expected loyally to serve all constitutional governments irrespective of party; the former, in return, are expected to accord their confidence to all civil servants, irrespective of their supposed party sympathies.

This also, to some extent, is a fiction. In Great Britain, where the civil service code is immensely potent, it is much more than a fiction, it is an almost universal fact. Other countries are less fortunate in the relations between their governments and the civil services.

The basic theory of democratic diplomacy is therefore as follows: "The diplomatist, being a civil servant, is subject to the Foreign Secretary; the Foreign Secretary, being a member of the Cabinet, is subject to the majority in Parliament; and Parliament, being but a representative Assembly, is subject to the will of the sovereign people."

Had these axioms been accepted and realized in 1918, much confusion of thought and action might have been prevented. The diplomatists, for their part, were not to blame, they did what they were told. But the public misconceived the true nature of the problem, and in their rightful desire to establish democratic control over what they carelessly called "diplomacy" they failed, as I have said, to make the essential distinction between policy, which was a legitimate subject for their control, and negotiation, which was not.

The anomalies which were created by this confusion can well be illustrated by the gulf which opened between the theories of President Wilson and his actions. Woodrow Wilson was the prophet of " open diplomacy," and in the first of the Fourteen Points which he promulgated on January 8, 1918, he laid it down that in future there should be " open covenants of peace openly arrived at, after which there shall be no private international understandings of any kind."

Less than a year after making this pronouncement, President Wilson was himself called upon to negotiate one of the most important covenants that have ever been concluded, namely the Treaty of Versailles. That treaty was certainly an open covenant since its terms were published before they were submitted to the approval of the sovereign authority in the several signatory States. Yet with equal certainty it was not " openly arrived at." In fact few negotiations in history have been so secret, or indeed so occult.

Not only were Germany and her allies excluded from any part in the discussion ; not only were all the minor Powers kept in the dark regarding the several stages of the negotiations ; not only were the press accorded no information beyond the most meagre of official bulletins ; but in the end President Wilson shut himself up in his own study with Lloyd George and Clemenceau, while an American marine with fixed bayonet marched up and down in order to prevent the intrusion of all experts, diplomatists or plenipotentiaries, including even the President's own colleagues on the American Delegation.

I am not contending for the moment that such secrecy was not inevitable, I am merely pointing out that it was unparalleled. It proves that the highest apostle of " open diplomacy " found, when it came to practice, that open negotiation was totally unworkable. And it shows how false was the position into which President Wilson (a gifted and in many ways a noble man) had placed himself, by having failed, in January 1918, to foresee that there was all the difference in the world between " open covenants " and " openly arrived at " —between policy and negotiation.

II

The ordinary citizen in democratic countries shared this illusion. He did not observe, for instance, that as a result of the Paris Conference, of the treaties which were then concluded, and of the practice which was thereafter established, he had in fact attained the very thing which he desired, namely democratic control of foreign policy. How was this admirable aim achieved ?

Until 1914 it was not generally realized that, even in countries which possessed ancient representative institutions, the control of foreign policy was not really vested in the elected representatives of the people. The terms of the Franco-Russian alliance, for instance, were not known either to the Russian or the French peoples, although in certain eventualities it committed those peoples to war or to a breach of national good faith. The exact nature of the Triple Alliance was hidden from the German, Austrian and the Italian public, although it was those very terms which dragged Germany into the war. And even so convinced a Liberal as Lord Grey of Fallodon saw nothing wrong in entering into engagements and making promises of which, not only the country, not only the two Houses of Parliament, but even the majority of the Cabinet, were unaware.

On realizing that they had in this manner been committed without their consent, the democracies of the world determined that this should not happen again. Two essential steps were taken to prevent a recurrence of such a situation. But as the public by then were prancing off after the red herrings of "secret diplomacy" and "openly arrived at" they failed to realize what a revolution, by these two measures, had been effected in the direction of democratic control.

The first measure was a provision inserted as Article 18 in the Covenant of the League of Nations. It reads as follows:

" Every treaty or international engagement entered into hereafter by any Member of the League shall be forthwith registered with the Secretariat and shall as soon as possible be published by it. No such treaty or international engagement shall be binding until so registered."

This provision would, if all the Powers of the world had become or had remained members of the League of Nations, have effectively put an end to all secret treaties, and with them to all secret foreign policy, of a nature to commit peoples to war without their knowledge. Unfortunately abstentions and defections from membership have left outside many countries, who are now at liberty to conclude secret treaties as between themselves. Yet the peoples of countries who are still members of the League have the assurance that no secret treaty signed by their governments has any legal validity unless it be published; and in this way they for their part are safeguarded against such situations as arose in 1914.

The second step which has been taken to ensure democratic control of policy is a definite alteration (again in democratic countries only) of the former theory and practice of " ratification." By ratification is meant the final approval given by the sovereign authority in a country to the treaties concluded by its representatives.

Before 1918 ratification was little more than a conventional formula. The government of the day, possessing a majority in Parliament, furnished certain envoys or negotiators with "full powers" to sign a given treaty and with instructions regarding the aims which it was desired to achieve and the concessions that the government might, if necessary, be prepared to make. Provided that the negotiator faithfully executed his instructions the treaty which he signed was ratified as a matter of course. There might (as in the case of the Anglo-Russian convention of 1907) be some debate, and some acrid criticism, regarding the actual terms of the treaty. Yet in all European countries at least, the government of the day regarded themselves as morally pledged by the signature of their plenipotentiaries; a repudiation of that signature, or in other words a denial of ratification, would have been regarded as implying a vote of non-confidence and would thereby have entailed the resignation of the government in power. Moreover, until 1919, such action on the part of a European Power would have seemed an act of international bad faith and a violation of the principles of the Concert of Europe.

It should be noted, incidentally, that the practice of the United States had always been different. Under Section 2 of Article II of the Constitution, the power of ratification is vested in the President

" by and with the advice " of a two-thirds majority of the Senate. It has thus not infrequently happened that the Senators have either refused to ratify a treaty or have insisted on adding bright ideas of their own. When, in 1807, the Senate sent back the Treaty of London unratified and asked for further alteration Canning described their action as " a practice altogether unusual in the political transactions of States." Yet in this unusual practice the Senate have persisted ever since. And the most resounding example of their theory and powers was provided by the refusal to ratify a treaty which had been signed and negotiated by the President in person. I refer to the Treaty of Versailles.

A profound effect was created in Europe by this refusal. Although it flung the whole peace settlement into chaos, it assuredly led other countries to realize that in this formality of ratification lay the solution of democratic control. To-day the ratification of any treaty concluded by a democratic government is actually, and not merely technically, subject to the approval of a majority of the Houses of Parliament. And in order to reinforce this safeguard, the first Labour Government in Great Britain established the rule that any treaty requiring ratification must lie upon the table of the House for at least twenty-one days before being ratified.

Although these provisions do in fact constitute

a tremendous safeguard against secret treaties or secret policy, and although they represent the veritable buttress of democratic control, the present system cannot in any sense be regarded as a final solution. It is in fact highly inconvenient and inefficient. It is obvious that the whole process of negotiation will be much encumbered if the negotiator on each side is totally unable to guarantee that what he gives or takes will be accepted by the sovereign authority in his own country. In the old days, European diplomacy did not, except in rare and exceptional circumstances, have to face this problem. Thus while the new practice represents an immense gain in the direction of "open covenants" it is a terrible liability in respect of negotiation.

The art of negotiation is severely hampered when one powerful negotiator demands concessions from his fellow negotiators without being in a position to guarantee that his own promises will similarly be fulfilled. If democratic diplomacy is to prove as efficient as its predecessors, this is one of the problems which it will have to solve.

III

It is not the only problem. Every system of government has its peculiar virtues and its peculiar faults, which in their turn affect foreign policy and the machinery by which it is executed. If we admit that one of the great achievements of democratic diplomacy is to have abolished the pernicious system of secret treaties, we must also admit that it has introduced other complications which hamper, not merely the art of negotiation, but also the amity and stability of international relations.

What, therefore, are the particular dangers or difficulties to which democratic diplomacy is exposed both in its theory and in its practice? I shall begin with theory.

It will be generally agreed that the most potent source of danger in democratic diplomacy is the irresponsibility of the sovereign people. By this I mean that, although the people are now the sovereign authority which ultimately controls foreign policy, yet they are almost wholly unaware of the responsibilities which this entails.

In the days of absolute monarchy the personal honour of the King was involved in the maintenance of the contracts or treaties which had been signed and ratified in his name. Monarchs were not invariably very sensitive to this obligation, but they were at least aware (and Louis XIV was constantly aware) that their own reputation for integrity was directly and personally at stake. Similarly, when the control of policy shifted from the individual monarch to a governing class, the feeling persisted that the engagements entered into by the government pledged the honour of the class as a whole. Yet now that the innumerable anonymous and unconscious electorate control foreign policy, this sense of personal, or corporate responsibility no longer exists. The sovereign people are not conscious of their sovereignty and are therefore unaware that it is they themselves who have caused these treaties to be signed.

This irresponsibility is encouraged by certain popular newspapers, which are apt to advocate the repudiation of pledges without even mentioning that such pledges have been incurred by a duly elected government, and ratified, after full discussion, by both Houses of Parliament. The same newspaper proprietor who would be profoundly shocked were an advertising firm or a news-print manufacturer to repudiate their contracts, is perfectly prepared to preach similar repudiation to the country as a whole.

Were it to become the practice of democracies to disavow the decisions which have been come to in their name and endorsed by their representatives, then clearly the whole basis of international contract would be destroyed ; anarchy would follow.

This problem is closely connected with the second great danger of democratic diplomacy, namely ignorance. By "ignorance" I do not mean ignorance of ascertainable facts ; it is the duty of their rulers and experts to provide the electorate with the essential facts in digestible form. It matters little whether the electorate know where Teschen is or what is the output of the Skoda works. But it does matter greatly that in their approach to foreign affairs the democracies of the world do not all of them manifest that balance and good sense which they apply to domestic problems.

Thus, even educated electors are almost totally unaware what are to-day the treaties by which their countries are bound. These treaties have been published, debated in Parliament and discussed in the press. Yet the vast majority of the people have no conception of their existence, have forgotten all about them, and would certainly clamour about " secret diplomacy " once they were invoked. It is only when the honouring of our national engagements becomes a matter of topical concern that the public remember, or even learn of, their existence. It is at that stage, when it is too late, that the sovereign people clamour for the abrogation of contracts of which they had themselves approved.

Nor is this all. The ordinary elector is not merely ignorant, lazy and forgetful regarding the international commitments for which he has himself assumed responsibility, but he does not apply to the general theory of foreign affairs that thought and intelligence which he devotes to domestic matters. He is unwilling to make any effort of comprehension or to try to understand the simplest elements of the problem.

In Great Britain, for instance, the ordinary man or woman has not yet realized that foreign affairs are *foreign* affairs, namely that they concern, not our own national interests only, but also the interests of other countries. They imagine that a foreign policy is framed in much the same manner as a budget or an education bill. That it is prepared by the responsible Minister, submitted to the Cabinet, approved by Parliament, and that thereafter all that remains to be done is to hand it over to the Foreign Office for execution. This confusion of thought tempts them to believe that an ideal foreign policy for Great Britain has only to be devised in order to be carried out. They ignore the fact that other countries, with equally powerful armaments, interests and prejudices, must similarly be consulted if any policy is to be effective.

The extent of this ignorance, the narcotic force of ill-considered slogans, can be well illustrated by two enquiries which I myself received. The first was, " Why does not the Government enter into an offensive alliance with the United States ? " The second was, " Why does the Government not understand that what the country wants is collective security and the League of Nations ; and that they will never stand for any European entanglements ? " The foolishness of such enquiries leads one at moments to despair of democratic diplomacy.

More dangerous even than popular ignorance, are certain forms of popular knowledge. The professional diplomatist, having spent his life in studying the psychology and conditions of foreign countries, is very chary of basing generalizations upon hastily observed phenomena. The elector shows no such hesitation. A summer cruise to Dalmatia, a bicycling tour in the Black Forest, three happy weeks at Porto Fino, and he returns equipped with certain profound convictions regarding the Near East, the relations between Herr Hitler and his General Staff, and the effect of the Abyssinian venture upon Italian public opinion. Since his judgment is based upon feelings rather than upon thoughts, he is at the mercy of any chance encounter or any accidental conversation. The fact that some impatient policeman may have pushed or prodded Effie that day at Hildesheim may well render Effie's parents " anti-German " for life. The fact that the hotel porter at Ragusa presented Arthur with three interesting pre-war postage stamps, may well convince Arthur's father that the Jugo-Slavs are the kindliest and most gentle race on earth. A slight controversy with the *ouvreuse* of a Paris theatre may, within the space of five minutes, turn a British citizen into a passionate Francophobe. Even such accidents as bad weather or a missed railway connection may permanently influence an elector's attitude towards foreign affairs. Such effects are not the least disturbing symptoms of democratic irresponsibility.

IV

A third danger is the danger of delay. An absolute monarch or a dictator can frame and execute a policy within the space of a few hours. A democratic government has to wait until public opinion has digested its own conclusions. True it is that these conclusions, when reached, are generally more sensible and more stable than the somnambulist certainties of a dictator. Yet the months which must elapse before any definite public opinion can be ascertained is often fatal to efficient policy or negotiation.

This time-lag between the convictions of the experts and the assent of the ordinary elector is a disadvantage which would seem inseparable from all forms of democratic diplomacy. Let me give an instance. By January 1919 Mr. Lloyd George had been convinced by his financial experts that it would be prejudicial to our own interests to extract from Germany an indemnity so large as to render bankrupt our best customer or to cause disturbances in international exchange such as would damage our economy. Yet the British public and the House of Commons took eighteen months to reach a similar conclusion. French public opinion took five years. As a result, the whole German middle classes were reduced to ruin and hopelessness, with the consequences which we are all sadly witnessing to-day.

A fourth danger which lies in wait for democratic diplomacy is the danger of imprecision. The vagueness and fluidity of democratic policy is one of its most salient vices. Not only is there the uncertainty which arises from the irresponsible attitude adopted by sovereign democracy towards its own obligations, but there is the tendency of all democracies (and especially of Anglo-Saxon democracies) to prefer a vague and comforting formula to a precise and binding definition. The effectiveness of any diplomacy is dependent upon the amount of conviction or certainty that it inspires; yet if policy be non-committal, then its servant diplomacy must also be vague. Thus it often occurs that democratic governments, by couching their statements of policy in vague or ambiguous language, invite the very dangers which they wish to prevent.

Nor is imprecision the only temptation to which a democratic statesman or diplomatist is exposed. In order that his policy may make an appeal to the ordinary man or woman he is apt to emphasize the emotional, dramatic or moral aspects of the situation and to suppress the practical aspects.

In extreme cases this leads him into actual hypocrisy, as when, in defending vital national interests, he pretends that he is defending some abstract idea. This temptation is one to which British statesmen all too readily succumb.

V

The above considerations have mainly centred upon those changes in diplomatic theory which have been occasioned by democratic control of foreign policy. New problems have also arisen in regard to diplomatic practice.

The first problem is that of publicity, since obviously the sovereign democracy needs to be informed. The use of the printing press as an ally to diplomacy is as old as Swift and the Treaty of Utrecht. Canning and Palmerston, as we have seen, believed fervently in an instructed public opinion, and enormous influence was exercised during the later nineteenth century by such newspapers as *The Times*. Cavour in Italy and Bismarck in Germany employed the Press for the purposes of secret rather than of open diplomacy, and Bismarck himself was not above fabricating articles and letters which served the uses of his policy.

The present problem is of a different nature. In the dictator States the controlled Press is used as a vehicle of propaganda. In democratic countries the aim is to employ it for purposes of information and education. Yet a satisfactory adjustment between the needs and rights of a popular Press and the requirements of discretion has yet to be found. In Great Britain, where the Press has a fine sense of responsibility, and an even finer sense of independence, the problem has not as yet become acute. In other countries, where the Press may be venal and is often sensational, publicity has proved the enemy rather than the friend of sensible diplomacy.

Before the war the problem of publicity was dealt with by European diplomatists in different ways. It was, and still is, customary upon the continent for the Foreign Minister or Foreign Office to favour certain special newspaper or agency; these are called, politely, " the inspired press "; or, less politely, the " reptile press." In Great Britain the custom was to differentiate rather vaguely between the " responsible " and the " irresponsible " newspapers, the latter category representing those journals which were not too friendly to the government. With the advent of democratic diplomacy this system of newspaper favouritism obviously became impossible, and even in Downing Street a Press Department was installed.

The present British system, although by no means fool-proof, works well enough. In so far as " news " is concerned a loyal attempt is made not to discriminate between any of the newspapers. In so far as " guidance " is concerned, it is obvious that certain correspondents (whether serving government or opposition papers) are more experienced, intelligent and reliable than other correspondents. It is inevitable that the former should be treated with greater confidence than the latter. Nor has the system in practice aroused serious discontent.

Far more complicated than the actual relations between the Press and the Foreign Office, is the effect of a free Press upon continental opinion. Foreign governments do not really believe that the British Press is as independent of the Foreign Office as is actually the case. If *The Times* writes a leading article which appears to differ from official policy, foreign observers do not believe that Printing House Square has had a sharp brain-wave all on its own, they believe that the Foreign Office is "flying a kite." Similarly, if one or other of the great national dailies launch an attack upon the Government, foreign observers tend to imagine that the latter is "testing public opinion." This misconception leads to many disadvantages. On the one hand it tempts other governments to conclude that British opinion is more divided, or the Government more undecided than they actually are. And on the other hand it leads them to blame the Foreign Office for attacks upon foreign countries or personalities which that unfortunate department is honestly quite unable to control.

The advantages of a free Press are so immeasurably greater than its disadvantages that this particular problem of democratic diplomacy need not cause anxiety. It is little more than a minor inconvenience.

A more dangerous innovation in diplomatic practice is the tendency of democratic countries to allow their politicians to take a personal part in negotiation. Clearly there are moments when it is essential that the Prime Minister or the Foreign Minister should attend important conferences. Yet repeated personal visits on the part of the Foreign Secretary of one country to the Foreign Secretary of the other should not be encouraged. Such visits arouse public expectation, lead to misunderstandings, and create confusion. The time at the disposal of these visitors is not always sufficient to allow for patience and calm deliberation. The honours which are paid to a minister in a foreign capital may tire his physique, excite his vanity, or bewilder his judgment. His desire not to offend his host may lead him, with lamentable results, to avoid raising unpalatable questions or to be imprecise regarding acute points of controversy. Nor is he always able on his return to obtain the approval of his Cabinet colleagues to his statements and actions.

Such visits, naturally enough, are very dear to the heart of all politicians. They are called "the value of personal contact." Yet in truth, as I have said elsewhere, diplomacy is not the art of conversation, it is the art of negotiating agreements in precise and ratifiable form. As such, it is, on all ordinary occasions, far better left to the professional diplomatist. His visits to the Foreign Office of the government to which he is accredited arouse no public expectation, inspire no Press indiscretions, and if sterile lead to no public disappointment. He has ample time to renew his visits at regular intervals and to occupy the intervening weeks or days in informing his government, obtaining instructions, and pondering tranquilly upon the negotiation itself. He is not hampered by ceremonial, or embarrassed by excessive courtesy. And above all the stages and results of his negotiation are carefully recorded in written documents.

VI

Such are some of the main problems in theory and practice which diplomacy under a democratic system has yet to solve. I do not wish to leave in the mind of the reader the impression that I regard democratic diplomacy as more inefficient or dangerous than its predecessors. Far from it. I consider it, even in its present confused state, infinitely preferable to any other system. Yet I confess that to my mind democratic diplomacy has not as yet discovered its own formula.

How is that formula to be found? It will only be by long processes of trial and error that we can hope to adjust this infinitely delicate piano to the sturdy fingers of a popular electorate. Yet there are certain principles of adjustment which it may be well to bear in mind.

It is in the first place important that the electorate should come to realize the distinction, on which I have dwelt so heavily, between policy and negotiation. Once they fully understand that they are safeguarded against secret policy, they may not worry themselves so acutely over the imaginary terrors of secret negotiation.

In the second place, once confidence has been re-established between diplomacy and its sovereign, it is important that the professional side of diplomacy should be fortified and its basis enlarged. It is possible in future years that we may have as foreign secretaries or prime ministers men who, owing to lack of experience, take an emotional or sentimental view of foreign policy. It is essential that such men should be able to call upon the services of a thoroughly experienced staff. Yet that staff must also be democratized and must cease to be generally, although to some extent inaccurately, regarded as the preserve of the upper bourgeoisie.

And in the third place nothing should be left undone to educate the public, not so much in regard to the details of foreign affairs, as in regard to those general principles of good sense and experience which have been evolved by generations of gifted and reasonable persons, and which, so long as men live in separate independent States, must always govern their relations between themselves.

CHAPTER V

THE IDEAL DIPLOMATIST

The principles which experience has shown to be necessary to sound diplomacy can well be illustrated by examining the qualities needed by the ideal diplomatist —What are these specific qualities ?—Some are now out of date—Others are still essential—The basis of good negotiation is moral influence and that influence is founded on seven specific diplomatic virtues, namely :—(1) Truthfulness—(2) Precision—(3) Calm—(4) Good temper—(5) Patience—(6) Modesty—(7) Loyalty

What are those " general principles of good sense and experience " to which, at the conclusion of the last chapter, I referred ? They can, I think, most conveniently be expounded if in this chapter I try to define the moral and intellectual qualities which the ideal diplomatist should possess. Yet if I catalogue these qualities in the shape of personal characteristics, I should not wish it to be supposed that I am indulging in a mere character sketch in the manner of Theophrastus or La Bruyère. My purpose is more practical than that. It is to illustrate by these qualities what rules and prescriptions sound diplomacy, in the passage of centuries, has evolved for itself. I wish at the same time to lay down certain standards of criticism by which the student of diplomacy may be able to judge what is "good diplomacy" and what is "bad diplomacy." And I hope thereby to indicate to the reader that the art of negotiation requires a combination of certain special qualities which are not always to be found in the ordinary politician, nor even in the ordinary man.

Most writers on diplomatic theory have devoted much space to a discussion of the qualities necessary for a successful negotiator. They are generally agreed that an ambassador, if he is to be successful, should be able to gain the confidence and liking of those exercising authority in the country to which he is accredited. This necessarily entails consideration both of time and of place. A man who might have made an admirable ambassador in the seventeenth century is unlikely to prove anything but a laughing-stock to-day. A man who had been eminently successful at Teheran might prove a ghastly failure if transferred to Washington. These differences are obvious and need not detain us. Yet before I pass to what I should call the permanent qualities of the negotiator it may be interesting to glance for a moment at those other qualities which were once thought necessary and which to-day no longer apply.

In the admirable article upon Diplomacy contributed to the *Encyclopædia Britannica* by Professor

Alison Phillips, some interesting extracts are given from former manuals defining the qualifications necessary for the ideal diplomatist. Ottaviano Maggi, for instance (whose *De Legato* was published in 1596), contended that an ambassador should be a trained theologian, should be well versed in Aristotle and Plato, and should be able at a moment's notice to solve the most abstruse problems in correct dialectical form : he should also be expert in mathematics, architecture, music, physics and civil and canon law. He should speak and write Latin fluently and must also be proficient in Greek, Spanish, French, German and Turkish. While being a trained classical scholar, a historian, a geographer and an expert in military science, he must also have a cultured taste for poetry. And above all he must be of excellent family, rich, and endowed with a fine physical presence.

More specific qualities were sometimes demanded. Thus we find the Princess of Zerbst, mother of the Empress Catherine of Russia, writing to Frederick the Great advising him to choose as his Ambassador to St. Petersburg a handsome young man with a good complexion ; whereas a capacity for absorbing without derangement vast quantities of intoxicating liquor was considered essential in any envoy to Holland or the German Courts.

These qualifications are no longer regarded as

absolutely essential by those who nominate candidates for the Diplomatic Examination. It might be said even that the old theory of selecting a certain type of personality for a certain type of post is falling into disrepute and being succeeded by the idea that a man who has proved himself efficient in one country is likely on the whole to be equally efficient in another. Experience has shown that there is much truth in this contention and that intelligence and character are equally effective in Warsaw as they are in Buenos Aires. It is sometimes said, however, that the British Foreign Office press this idea too far and are apt to make their appointments without regard to the psychology of the individual or the conditions of the post to which he is being sent. Such a criticism is, on the whole, unfounded.

It is interesting also to observe that throughout the ages opinions have differed on the question whether intelligence or character, cunning or probity, are the more effective instruments of diplomacy. Even some quite modern diplomatists have sought to justify the diplomatic lie. Thus Prince Bülow contended that Bethmann-Hollweg should have flatly denied that he ever used that unfortunate phrase about "a scrap of paper." Count Szilassy, in his treatise on diplomacy, definitely argues that in certain circumstances it is "patriotic" to tell a deliberate falsehood. Such writers are not representative of classic diplomatic theory. Count Szilassy was a very minor diplomatist, whereas Prince Bülow was the most disastrous statesman that even Germany has ever possessed. The general trend of opinion upon the art of negotiation has been markedly in favour of "credit" and "confidence" in preference to deception. Nor is this more enlightened conception merely a product of comparatively recent times.

Monsieur de Callières, for instance, published in 1716 a treatise entitled: "*On the manner of negotiation with Princes; on the uses of diplomacy; the choice of ministers and envoys; and the personal qualities necessary for success in missions abroad.*" This manual, which was regarded as a text-book by eighteenth-century diplomatists, contains many wise and righteous precepts, some of which I shall quote in the pages that follow. For the moment I shall only reproduce the following passage as indicating that, even at a time when Frederick the Great was four years old, the Bülow theory of diplomacy made no appeal to men of common sense.

"The good negotiator," writes de Callières, "will never base the success of his negotiations upon false promises or breaches of faith; it is an error to suppose, as public opinion supposes, that it is necessary for an efficient Ambassador to be a past master in the art of deception; dishonesty is in fact little more than a proof of the smallness of mind of he who resorts to it, and shows that he is too meagrely equipped to gain his purposes by just and reasonable methods. Doubtless the art of lying has on occasions been successfully practised by diplomatists; but unlike that honesty which here, as elsewhere, is the best policy, a lie always leaves in its wake a drop of poison. . . . Even the most dazzling diplomatic triumphs which have been gained by deception are based upon insecure foundations. They leave the defeated party with a sense of indignation, a desire to be revenged and a resentment which will always be a danger.

Even were deceit not in itself repugnant to every right-minded person, the negotiator should recollect that he is likely for the rest of his life to be constantly engaged in diplomatic business, and that it is essential for him to establish a reputation for straight and honest dealing so that thereafter men may be ready to trust his word."

II

It will be evident from the above that even in the eighteenth century diplomatists who put down on paper the results of their own experience placed moral integrity in the forefront of the qualities which a successful diplomatist must possess. M.

Jules Cambon, writing more than two-hundred years after Callières, was of the same opinion.

"It will be seen," he writes, "that moral influence is the most essential qualification of a diplomatist. He must be a man of the strictest honour if the government to which he is accredited and his own government are to place explicit confidence in his statements."

If therefore we admit that the ingenious diplomatist is likely to prove the unreliable diplomatist and that the unreliable diplomatist is certain to be a dangerous failure—then we must examine what special virtues, under the general heading of "moral influence," our ideal diplomatist must either possess or acquire.

First among these virtues is truthfulness. By this is meant, not merely abstention from conscious misstatements, but a scrupulous care to avoid the suggestion of the false or the suppression of the true. A good diplomatist should be at pains not to leave any incorrect impressions whatsoever upon the minds of those with whom he negotiates. If, in perfect good faith, he misleads a foreign minister, or if subsequent information contradicts information which he had previously communicated, he should at once correct the misapprehension, however temporarily convenient it may seem to allow it to remain. Even if we judge negotiation by its lowest standards, it is evident that the correction of inaccurate information increases present credit and fortifies future confidence.

Nor should the negotiator for one moment allow himself to agree with Machiavelli that the dishonesty of others justifies any dishonesty in oneself. Baron Sonnino, Italian Foreign Minister in 1918, caused to be carved upon the mantelpiece of his study the motto " *Aliis licet : tibi non licet*,"— " others may : you mayn't." That motto should be borne in mind by all diplomatists.

A similar rule is applicable to those who have to deal with the subtleties of the Oriental mind. A notable British diplomatist, who had long experience in the Far and Middle East, was in the habit of providing younger negotiators appointed to Oriental capitals with the following piece of advice : " Do not waste your time in trying to discover what is at the back of an Oriental's mind ; there may, for all you know, be nothing at the back ; concentrate all your attention upon making quite certain that he is left in no doubt whatsoever in regard to what is at the back of *your* mind."

The principle that truthfulness is essential to any efficient diplomacy is, as I have said above, no very recent discovery. I have already referred to Lord Malmesbury as an example of the old diplomacy and have described his methods. Yet even Lord Malmesbury learnt by experience that duplicity simply did not pay. Writing to Lord Camden in 1813, in response to a request for his opinion regarding diplomatic conduct, he expressed himself as follows:

"It is scarcely necessary to say that no occasion, no provocation, no anxiety to rebut an unjust accusation, no idea—however tempting—of promoting the object you have in view—can *need*, much less justify, a *falsehood*. Success obtained by one is a precarious and baseless success. Detection would ruin, not only your own reputation for ever, but deeply wound the honour of your Court. If, as frequently happens, an indiscreet question, which seems to require a distinct answer, is put to you abruptly by an artful minister, parry it either by treating it as an indiscreet question, or get rid of it by a grave and serious look; but on no account contradict the assertion flatly if it be true, or admit it as true, if false and of a dangerous tendency."

III

If truthfulness be the first essential for the ideal diplomatist, the second essential is precision. By this is meant not merely intellectual accuracy, but moral accuracy. The negotiator should be accurate both in mind and soul.

The professional diplomatist is inured, from his earliest days as an attaché, to rules of precision.

It is the amateur diplomatist who is apt to be slovenly. Even politicians, even cabinet ministers, have been known to overlook the fact that diplomacy, as its name implies, is a written rather than a verbal art and the great high-roads of history are strewn with little shrines of peace which have either been left unfinished, or have collapsed when completed, for the sole reason that their foundations were built on the sands of some verbal misconception. Björkoe, Buchlau, Thoiry, Stresa, Munich—these ruined temples should serve as warnings to all young negotiators.

Professional diplomacy is not, as a rule, so liable to imprecision. An ambassador almost invariably receives his instructions in writing; the representations which he thereafter makes to the foreign government are either embodied in a carefully drafted Note or conveyed in a personal interview; in the latter event he is careful, immediately on his return, to record the course of that interview in a despatch to his own government.

It is customary, moreover, when an ambassador has to make to a foreign government a communication of special importance that he should bring with him a short synopsis or *aide-mémoire* of what he is instructed to say. He may read this memorandum out to the foreign minister and he may also leave a copy behind. Conversely, when an ambassador receives from a foreign minister some vitally important oral communication, it is a wise precaution on his part to submit to the latter his version of the conversation before reporting it officially to his own government. Failure to take this precaution has led to regrettable incidents in the past. A classic instance of such a misunderstanding is the repudiation by M. Guizot in 1848 of promises made verbally to Lord Normanby (then British Ambassador in Paris) and which the latter had reported in a despatch to London. M. Guizot stated that Lord Normanby had completely misinterpreted his remarks and that he had never made any promises of the nature asserted. He added the wise dictum that the report of a conversation furnished by an ambassador to his home government could only be regarded as authentic and binding if previously submitted for observations to the person whose statements it is supposed to represent.

Yet, although the professional diplomatist is seldom guilty of what I have called "intellectual inaccuracy," his temptation to what I have called "moral inaccuracy" is persistent and extreme.

This moral inaccuracy takes several forms. The experienced diplomatist is well aware that human actions are at the mercy of chance occurrences and that prophecy is always dangerous. He is thus tempted, if not to avoid all predictions, then at least to phrase his forecasts in a Delphic style.

The spirit, as well as the ingenious diction, of the Sibyl all too often furnish an example for the anxious diplomatist. He prefers to hedge. Justified, though he assuredly is, in avoiding all rash prophecies, as all intemperate statements, yet a diplomatist should not hesitate to inform his government of the direction in which he himself believes local events are likely to develop. The " heads I win, tails you lose " type of despatch may, it is true, enable an ambassador, after the event, to claim prescience by recalling his previous reference either to tails or to heads ; yet it is not of deep benefit either to his government or to his own reputation. All too often diplomatists are so afraid of being accused of lack of judgment, that they avoid expressing any judgment at all. In evading these responsibilities they are omitting to perform one of their most desirable duties.

This is perhaps only a negative failing, but if this tendency towards moral imprecision affects an envoy's communications with the government to which he is accredited, then most serious damage may be done. An ambassador is rightly preoccupied with the task of maintaining friendly relations with the authorities with whom he has to deal. At times this preoccupation becomes excessive. It not infrequently occurs that a diplomatist, when instructed by his government to make a communication which he knows will cause irritation and pain, so waters down his instructions that an inaccurate and flaccid impression of their purport is conveyed.

Even if he be sufficiently loyal and conscientious to carry out the strict letter of his instructions, he is sometimes tempted, in order to avoid giving offence, to accompany the delivery of these instructions with such intonation of voice, such conciliation of gesture, as to imply that he himself does not really agree with the intimation which he has been instructed to make. These temptations, and their attendant symptoms, will be referred to again under the heading of "loyalty."

IV

A third quality which is essential to the ideal diplomatist is the quality of calm. Not only must the negotiator avoid displaying irritation when confronted by the stupidity, dishonesty, brutality or conceit of those with whom it is his unpleasant duty to negotiate; but he must eschew all personal animosities, all personal predilections, all enthusiasms, prejudices, vanities, exaggerations, dramatizations, and moral indignations. The well-known epigram of Talleyrand, when asked to give advice to a young diplomatist, would be echoed by all experienced negotiators: "*Et surtout pas trop de zèle*," "And above everything, do not allow yourself to become excited about your work."

The impassivity which characterizes the ideal diplomatist may render him much disliked by his friends. In fact the manner of suspended judgment, of sceptical tolerance, of passionless detachment which denotes the trained diplomatist, is often taken by outside observers to suggest that he is conceited, lazy, stupid, or very very ill.

The quality of calm, as applied to the ideal diplomatist, should express itself in two major directions. In the first place he should be good-tempered, or at least he should be able to keep his ill-temper under perfect control. In the second place he should be quite exceptionally patient.

The occasions on which diplomatists have lost their tempers are remembered with horror by generations of their successors. Napoleon lost his temper with Metternich in the Marcolini Palace at Dresden on June 26, 1813, and flung his hat upon the carpet with the most unfortunate results. Sir Charles Euan Smith lost his temper with the Sultan of Morocco and tore up a treaty in the imperial presence. Count Tattenbach lost his temper at the Algeciras Conference and exposed his country to a grave diplomatic humiliation. Herr Stinnes lost his temper at Spa.

Patience and perseverance are also essential to any successful negotiator. M. Paul Cambon—one of the most successful diplomatists in modern history and French Ambassador in London for over twenty years—was a miracle of patience. He arrived in England at a time when Franco-British relations were strained almost to breaking point. When he left it, we were firm allies. Throughout those twenty years M. Paul Cambon waited. He was always conciliatory; he was invariably discreet; he was the soul of loyalty; and he was always there. His extraordinary capacity for seizing the right moment, his delicate "sense of occasion," the extreme dignity of his manner, rendered him by 1914 a man who was universally trusted and universally esteemed. Similar patience has not always been displayed by the envoys of other nations who have wished to secure some rapid triumph and to return home quickly bearing some brilliant result. All too often these impatient ambassadors have frightened the British bull-dog away from its bone.

The brother of Paul Cambon—M. Jules Cambon, French Ambassador in Berlin—in his attractive study of *The Diplomatist* puts patience among the first of diplomatic virtues. "Patience," he writes, "is an indispensable quality for the successful negotiator. The wind is bound to be contrary at times, and then one has to tack to get into port." And he then proceeds to cite as an instance of patience and perseverance his own negotiations with Kiderlen-Waechter before the war.

V

A diplomatist may be truthful, accurate, calm, patient and good-tempered, but he is not an ideal diplomatist unless he be also modest. The dangers of vanity in a negotiator can scarcely be exaggerated. It tempts him to disregard the advice or opinions of those who may have had longer experience of a country, or of a problem, than he possesses himself. It renders him vulnerable to the flattery or the attacks of those with whom he is negotiating. It encourages him to take too personal a view of the nature and purposes of his functions and in extreme cases to prefer a brilliant but undesirable triumph to some unostentatious but more prudent compromise. It leads him to boast of his victories and thereby to incur the hatred of those whom he has vanquished. It may prevent him, at some crucial moment, from confessing to his government that his predictions or his information were incorrect. It prompts him to incur or to provoke unnecessary friction over matters which are of purely social importance. It may cause him to offend by ostentation, snobbishness or ordinary vulgarity. It is at the root of all indiscretion and of most tactlessness. It lures its addicts into displaying their own verbal brilliance, and into such fatal diplomatic indulgences as irony, epigrams, insinuations, and the barbed reply. It may prevent an ambassador from admitting even to himself that he does not know Turkish, Persian, Chinese and Russian sufficiently to enable him, in any important matter, to dispense with the services of an interpreter. It may induce that terrible and frequent illusion of the professional diplomatist that his own post is the centre of the diplomatic universe and that the Foreign Office is both blind and obstinate in ignoring his advice. It may betray him, when entertaining visiting politicians or journalists, to speak with disloyalty and cleverness about his own foreign secretary. And it may bring in its train those other vices of imprecision, excitability, impatience, emotionalism and even untruthfulness. Of all diplomatic faults (and they are many) personal vanity is assuredly the most common and the most disadvantageous.

Among the misfortunes into which personal vanity drives the frail spirit of man there is one which has a more specific bearing upon the practice of negotiation. It is self-satisfaction. It leads first to a loss of adaptability, and second to a decline in imagination.

Diplomatists, especially those who are appointed to, and liable to remain in, smaller posts, are apt to pass by slow gradations from ordinary human vanity to an inordinate sense of their own importance. The whole apparatus of diplomatic life—the ceremonial, the court functions, the large houses, the lacqueys and the food—induces an increasing sclerosis of personality. Such people, as they become older, incline to a slowness of speech, movement and perception which is almost akin to pompousness. The type of M. de Norpois is not, it is true, a common type in modern diplomacy. But, if it is unfair to take him as a sample, it is wise to regard him as a warning.

It is this rigidity of spirit which, as it settles upon the less gifted diplomatist, deprives him of his adaptability. He fails to respond with his former elasticity to conditions of which he disapproves or to ideas with which he is not familiar. This fault is of course common to all those who surrender themselves without a struggle to later middle age. Yet in a diplomatist it entails a real diminution of efficiency, since adaptability—or the power of putting oneself in another's place—is an essential element in successful negotiation.

Let me once again quote Callières :

" It is essential that a negotiator should be able to divest himself of his own opinion in order to place himself in the position of the Prince with whom he is negotiating. He should be able, that is, to adopt the other's personality, and to enter into his views and inclinations. And he should thus say to himself—' If I were in the place of that Prince, endowed with equal power, governed by identical prejudices and passions, what effect would my own representations make upon myself?'"

With loss of adaptability comes loss of imagination. In a young diplomatist, imagination is often a snare. "*Pas de fantaisie*" was the advice given (fruitlessly we may suppose) by the elder Bülow to his more famous son. Yet, if an older diplomatist loses his gift of imagination, he becomes all keel and ballast without sail. He fails to respond to the new winds which may blow from his own country, or to the squalls which may arise suddenly in the country where he is stationed. He becomes so satisfied with himself that he loses his former interest in the psychology of others. And since psychological alertness is one of the most vital factors in negotiation, a diplomatist who becomes lethargic in such matters has passed the period of usefulness.

Let me conclude this chapter with the seventh great virtue of the ideal diplomatist. It is the virtue of loyalty.

The professional diplomatist is governed by several different, and at times conflicting, loyalties. He owes loyalty to his own sovereign, government, minister and foreign office; he owes loyalty to his own staff; he owes a form of loyalty to the diplomatic body in the capital where he resides; he owes loyalty to the local British colony and its commercial interests ; and he owes another form of loyalty to the government to which he is accredited and to the minister with whom he negotiates.

There is always a tendency among diplomatists who have resided for long in foreign countries, and who have perhaps fallen out of contact with their own people and with their own foreign office, to find that their loyalties become a trifle blurred. They are apt either to love the country in which they reside with a sentimental passion which blinds them to all its vices, or else to loathe it with an intensity which is impervious to all its virtues. Alternatively they may have become so impressed by the doctrine that the function of an ambassador is to create " good relations " with a foreign government, that they confuse the end with the means, and see " good relations " not as part of their functions but as the sole purpose of their activity. Their intense concentration upon the work of their own mission may blind them to the fact that their own country does in fact possess missions in other capitals as well, and that the only central authority which is in possession of all sources of information and which is able to balance correctly the diplomatic position in one country against that in another, is the Foreign Office at home. Personal antipathy to some foreign colleague may diminish their readiness to co-operate with that colleague even when co-operation is the policy of the two countries which they represent. Old traditions, old rivalries even, may make it obnoxious to them to execute full-heartedly some new policy which a Foreign Secretary may advocate. And occasionally, even, personal friction with his staff may divert the attention of an envoy from the more serious business of his mission.

To all such poisons which may attack the negotiator there is one sovereign antidote. That antidote is loyalty above all to the government whom he serves.

I have previously indicated how easy it is for a diplomatist who finds himself in disagreement with the policy of his government to indicate that disagreement without violating the strict letter of his instructions. Yet even if he " assents with civil leer " he should know full well that his attitude is in fact an act of silent disloyalty.

A more subtle and unconscious disloyalty may intrude into the reports which he himself sends home. Even Callières warned the diplomatist against the temptation of telling his own government what they would *like* to hear, rather than what they *ought* to know. The most honourable envoy is liable to slide into this temptation without realizing that by so doing he is in fact committing an act of disloyalty towards his own government, who should be told the bitter truth.

Yet how tempting it is, for a diplomatist abroad,

while not departing from veracity, to make the most of all favourable fact! He knows that his despatches will reach Downing Street or the Quai d'Orsay at the same time as other despatches from other capitals. He also knows that the Foreign Office officials who have to read and minute these despatches are overwhelmed with work and burdened with anxiety. He knows that (human nature being as it is) a comforting despatch arouses feelings of pleasure, whereas a disturbing despatch causes pangs of pain. Inevitably the harassed official who finds upon his table six despatches coming from six different countries is distressed by sharp criticisms of inertia at home or gloomy forebodings of trouble in the future. He turns with relief from the despatch of Sir Charles X . . . (who writes, " Unless you take urgent and immediate action complete catastrophe will result ") to the despatch of Sir Henry Y . . . (who writes, " Owing to the vigour and foresight manifested by His Majesty's Government the situation is now completely in hand; you may leave everything to me, I need no further instructions ").

Inevitably the harassed official comes to the conclusion that Sir Charles X . . . is " cantankerous and wrong-headed," whereas Sir Henry Y . . . is " definitely a reliable man." And here again François Callières, so long ago as 1716, uttered his warning.

These, then, are the qualities of my ideal diplomatist. Truth, accuracy, calm, patience, good temper, modesty and loyalty. They are also the qualities of an ideal diplomacy.

" But," the reader may object, " you have forgotten intelligence, knowledge, discernment, prudence, hospitality, charm, industry, courage and even tact." I have not forgotten them. I have taken them for granted.

CHAPTER VI

TYPES OF EUROPEAN DIPLOMACY

Amateurishness of British and American politicians—American Diplomacy—British Diplomacy—A reflection of policy—Foundations of British policy—The Eyre Crowe memorandum—The Balance of Power—Certain precepts of British policy—How do these affect British diplomacy ?—Virtues and vices of British diplomatic method—Criticisms made by foreign observers—The relation between caution and timidity—German political theory—From Fichte to Hitler—The cult of the State and the mystic belief in force as a unifying formula—Effect of this theory upon diplomatic practice—Sudden diplomacy—Fear versus conciliation—French policy and diplomacy—Faults of the French system—Rigidity and intolerance—The Italian conception of mobility—Italian methods—Great Power versus Small Power diplomacy

In preceding chapters I have emphasized the continuity of diplomatic practice and theory and have tried to show that there exist certain standards of negotiation which might be regarded as permanent and universal. Apart from these standards, which should be common to all diplomacy, there are marked differences in the theory and practice of the several Great Powers. These differences are caused by variations in national character, traditions and requirements. One can thus distinguish types, or species, of diplomacy and it is important that these distinctions should be recognized. All diplomatists (the professionals scarcely less than the amateurs) are inclined to assume that their own conception of the art of negotiation is shared more or less by those foreigners with whom they are negotiating. This fallacy leads to misunderstanding.

It might be admitted, incidentally, that British statesmen are peculiarly prone to this illusion. They are so accustomed, in domestic controversies, to invoke the principle of fair dealing and to rely upon settlement by compromise, that they do not understand that such conceptions are not always present in the minds of foreign negotiators. It was difficult, for instance, for those who worked under Sir Edward Grey to convince him that the envoy of some Balkan country did not possess the same sort of traditions, intuitions and principles, as he had inherited himself: he was inclined to regard them, if not perhaps as Old Wykehamists, then at least as Old Marlburians. If subsequent developments led him to revise this opinion, he would feel that a gross deception had been practised upon him, and would regard the foreign statesman who had failed to live up to Old Marlburian standards as a man of irredeemable iniquity.

The Americans, conversely, are convinced that all diplomatists are determined to ensnare, entangle and humiliate all those with whom they negotiate. They enter a conference as Daniel entered the den of lions, conscious that it is only their own bright faith and innocence which will preserve them from the claws of the wild beasts by whom they are surrounded. It is in fact strange that, whereas an American business man will negotiate with foreign business men in a spirit of almost reckless self-confidence, an American diplomatist will, in the presence of continental diplomatists, become overwhelmed with diffidence and suspicion. These errors, of British optimism and American pessimism, might be corrected were the differences in the diplomatic methods and standards of the several countries realized and accepted with greater clarity.

I propose therefore in the present chapter to examine the differences in diplomatic theory and practice which exist between Great Britain, Germany, France and Italy. I should extend my examination to a discussion of "Small Power Diplomacy" and "Oriental Diplomacy," were it not that the four main types which I have chosen will amply suffice to illustrate the distinctions which I wish to suggest.

I shall not discuss United States diplomacy, since it is only recently that a professional American foreign service has come into existence and since it has had no time to develop its particular technique. In past years the reputation of America's foreign service suffered much from the political appointments made under the "spoils system." A political supporter who was accorded the perquisite of an Embassy or a Legation was all too often more concerned with maintaining his publicity-value in his home-town than with serving the rights and interests of his own country abroad. The capitals of Europe and Latin America echoed with the indiscretions of these amateur diplomatists and much damage was done to all concerned. Now that the American people have, in their wisdom, seen that some form of professional diplomacy is desirable, we may be confident that it will rapidly become among the best in the world. My own experience of American negotiators has been uniformly happy. I have found them reasonable, resourceful, well-informed, accurate and immensely reliable. They are hampered by the same disabilities as are the British diplomatists in that they are obliged to consider the feelings of their people at home. Nor do I envy any American diplomatist the jealous and almost totally ignorant scrutiny of Senatorial Committees. But their ideals are the same as British ideals, only simpler and more unhampered. And their methods will assuredly be the same as those which, in the course of centuries, have always commended themselves to men of humanity and common sense.

I now pass to the differences which can be

observed in the theory and practice of the Great European Powers. These differences arise, as I have said, from variations in national tradition, character and needs. It is these which determine policy; and policy in its turn determines diplomatic methods. It might indeed be contended that there can be no such thing as distinct "Types of Diplomacy" or "Types of Policy." Yet in fact it is possible to identify certain constant characteristics in the art of negotiation as practised by the Great Powers; and it is these characteristics which I propose to examine in this chapter.

II

British diplomacy is generally regarded by foreign observers with bewildered, and sometimes with indignant, admiration. On the one hand they notice that professional British diplomatists display little initiative, take no pains to impress others with their intellectual brilliance, and are to all appearance unimaginative, uninformative, lethargic and slow. On the other hand it is impossible to ignore the fact that the British diplomatist is exceptionally well informed, manages to acquire and to retain the confidence of foreign governments, is imperturbable in times of crisis, and almost always succeeds.

Foreign critics are apt to explain this anomaly by many fantastic theories. Sometimes they will contend that the British diplomatist is a man of diabolical cunning who, under the disguise of stolid respectability, conceals a mind which is nimble and treacherous in the extreme. At other times they will swing round to the opposite pole and contend that the success of British diplomacy is due to the eternal moral principles upon which it is founded. At other times, and with greater justification, they will explain the contradiction between apparent British ineptitude and their evident success, by contending that a diplomacy which is backed by such enormous potential power must always be almost fool-proof. And there are moments of enlightenment when they recognize that the art of negotiation is essentially a mercantile art, and that the success of British diplomacy is to be explained by the fact that it is founded on the sound business principles of moderation, fair-dealing, reasonableness, credit, compromise, and a distrust of all surprises or sensational extremes.

Essentially, British diplomacy is but the expression, in terms of international contacts, of those principles of policy which, owing to history, geographical position, imperial responsibilities, liberal institutions and national character, have, in the course of centuries, been found best suited to British requirements. What are those principles?

On January 1, 1907, Sir Eyre Crowe, at that time head of the Western Department of the

Foreign Office, wrote for the Cabinet a confidential memorandum upon Anglo-German relations. That memorandum, which contains incidentally an acute analysis of German aims, embodies a careful definition of the historical principles of British policy.

Sir Eyre Crowe took as his axiom the incontestable premise that British policy was determined by geography. On the one hand you had a small island situated on the exposed flank of Europe. On the other hand you had a vast Empire stretching across the world. The law of self-preservation necessitated the maintenance of the food-supplies of the island and the safety of its communications with its Empire overseas. This dual necessity implied preponderance of sea-power against any possible enemy. The United States are not a possible enemy.

It is the corollary of this proposition which applies to my present argument. Sir Eyre Crowe argued that this maritime supremacy would, if pressed, arouse feelings of resentment and jealousy throughout the world. It must therefore be exercised with the utmost benevolence and with the minimum of provocation. It must be "closely identified with the primary and vital interests of a majority of other nations."

What were these primary interests? The first was independence; the second was trade. British policy must therefore maintain the open door and must at the same time display " a direct and positive interest in the independence of small nations." Great Britain must therefore recognize herself as " the natural enemy of any nation which threatened the independence of smaller countries." The doctrine of the " Balance of Power " thus assumed for Great Britain a peculiar form. It meant that she must be " opposed to the political dictatorship of the strongest single State or group of States at any given time." This opposition, Sir Eyre Crowe stated, was for Great Britain " a law of nature."

Historians may question the validity of the latter assumption and may contend that the British instinct for self-preservation is not aroused by the threat of some continental dictatorship as such, but only when such dictatorships threaten the Channel ports or the Empire's maritime communications. Yet they would accept his former premise, namely that it is a principle of policy, rather than any special human virtue, that makes Great Britain see herself as the champion of the rights of small nations. And they would agree that this necessity, coupled with a democratic system, has tended during the last hundred years to render British policy, and therefore British diplomacy, more " liberal " than those of certain other powers.

If, therefore, we accept this general formula, it is useful to examine how in the last century it has expressed itself in international affairs and what are the particular precepts of policy which can be recognized as most specifically British.

III

The constant motive or principle which runs through all British foreign policy is the principle of the Balance of Power. That principle has in recent years acquired a bad reputation and has been much misunderstood. It does not, as its critics suppose, imply that British policy is constantly directed towards organizing coalitions against whatever country may at any time be the strongest Power in Europe; it means that the general trend of policy is opposed to any single Power or group of Powers who may seek to use their strength in order to deprive other European countries of their liberty and independence. "The Balance of Power," wrote Lord John Russell in 1859, "in Europe means in effect the independence of its several States."

It is evident that the doctrine of the Balance of Power has imposed upon British policy a peculiar quality of empiricism, or even of opportunism. The British system is not governed, as is the policy of Germany and Italy, by any planned ambitions, even as it is not determined (as French policy is determined) by preoccupation with any hereditary enemy: it depends upon combinations of events.

"And how," inquired a visitor to Sans Souci

in 1768, " would Your Majesty define the English system ? "

" The English," snapped Frederick the Great, " *have* no system."

This opportunism is fortified by the temperamental insularity of the British character and necessitated by the democratic nature of British institutions. It is for this reason that for the last hundred years British statesmen have done their best to avoid any planned or long-term foreign policy and to eschew as far as possible all precise continental commitments.

Canning and Palmerston were equally opposed to laying down " fixed resolutions for eventual probabilities."

" It is not usual," wrote the latter to our Ambassador in Russia, " for England to enter into engagements with reference to cases which have not actually arisen, or which are not immediately in prospect ; and this for a plain reason. All formal engagements of the Crown, which involve the questions of peace and war, must be submitted to Parliament ; and Parliament might probably not approve of an engagement which should bind England prospectively to take up arms in a contingency which could not as yet be foreseen."

The general precept underlying this principle has never been more lucidly expressed than in the letter which Gladstone wrote to Queen Victoria on April 17, 1869:

"England should keep entire in her own hands the means of estimating her own obligations upon the various states of facts as they arise; she should not foreclose and narrow her own liberty of choice by declarations made to other Powers, in their real or supposed interests, of which they would claim to be at least joint interpreters; it is dangerous for her to assume alone an advanced and therefore isolated position, in regard to European controversies; come what may it is better for her to promise too little than too much; she should not encourage the weak by giving expectation of aid to resist the strong, but should rather seek to deter the strong by firm but moderate language from aggression of the weak; she should seek to develop and mature the action of a common, or public, or European opinion, as the best standing bulwark against wrong, but should beware of seeming to lay down the law of that opinion by her own authority, and thus running the risk of setting against her, and against right and justice, the general sentiment which ought to be, and generally would be, arrayed in their favour."

Such, for more than one hundred years, have been the directives of British foreign policy. It is possible, now that Great Britain may appear to have lost her invulnerability, that these principles may be modified. It is probable that the former policy of alternating isolation with intervention may have to be supplanted by some more planned system of collective security and that to this extent the old doctrine of the Balance of Power will be abandoned. Yet it may be questioned whether the final decision in warfare has yet passed from the sea to the air, and it may be suggested that for many years Great Britain should adhere, with only slight modifications, to her old traditions. Whether her position in international affairs should best be described as that of " the honest broker," " the final arbiter," " the world's peace-maker," " the *tertius gaudens* " or " The God in the machine," is a matter of individual opinion.

How do these general precepts of policy affect the methods of British diplomacy? It is that problem which must now be considered.

IV

In his interesting work, *The Spirit of British Policy*, Dr. Kantorowicz has analysed, from a foreigner's point of view, the guiding principles of the British system and their effect upon diplomacy. His analysis is flattering to British self-esteem. He catalogues as the main virtues of British diplomacy the three qualities of Chivalry, Objectivity and Humanitarianism. Its main defect appears to him to be that of Irrationality. He does not dwell with any insistence upon the opportunism of the British system or upon its fundamental selfishness. Yet he does recognize (since he is a scholarly and charitable observer) that British policy is all too apt to fluctuate between idealism and realism, between humanitarianism and self-interest; and he rightly admits that Great Britain's international reputation for hypocrisy, as well as the phrase "perfidious Albion," is due, not to any national insincerity, but to a national distaste for logic, and a national preference for dealing with situations after they have arisen rather than before they arise. In other words, the typical British approach to any international problem is one from the idealistic to the realistic. The first impulse is one of humanitarianism and it is only at a later stage that the motives of self-interest or of self-preservation come into play; this is apt to create some discrepancy between the purposes which are proclaimed at the outset of an international crisis and those which determine British policy at the end.

Not all foreign observers are as kindly as Dr. Kantorowicz. Heinrich Heine, for instance, described the English "as the most odious race that God in his wrath had ever created," and warned his contemporaries against "the treacherous and murderous intrigues of those Carthaginians of the North Sea." Yet Heine was at the time writing as a journalist and his diatribes, which had some influence in France and Germany, can be largely discounted as being of the nature of propaganda. It is more interesting to consider how the English system struck trained observers, such as Prince Bülow, Count Bernstorff and Count Mensdorff. These diplomatists defined the main difference between the British and the continental attitude to foreign affairs under two headings. The first was simplicity, amounting to childishness; the second was sentimentality.

In 1899 Prince Bülow paid a visit to Windsor and recorded his impressions in his diary:

"The English politicians do not know the Continent well. They do not know much more about conditions on the Continent than we know about conditions in Peru or Siam. Their general ideas, according to our standard, are somewhat naïve. There is something naïve in their unconscious egotism, but they have also a certain credulity. They are not prone to suspect really evil intentions. They are very quiet, rather indolent and very optimistic."

Count Mensdorff, for long Austrian Ambassador in London and a good friend to Britain, shared Prince Bülow's judgment.

"Most of the British Ministers," he wrote, "and politicians are far more ignorant, inexact and amateurish than we believe. A good deal that we interpret as deceit is in fact merely the result of ignorance and superficiality, and is due to carelessness and confusion. Almost without exception, they have no clear idea about foreign conditions."

To this charge of ignorance and muddle-headedness is added a complaint of British sentimentality. This complaint assumed a somewhat startling form in a letter written to Prince Bülow in 1904 by Count Bernstorff, subsequently German Ambassador at Washington, and at the time Counsellor of the German Embassy in London:

"In my humble opinion an improvement in the relation between the two countries might well be initiated by the conclusion of a treaty of arbitration with England. In the form which is customary nowadays, such treaties are quite harmless and *de facto* of no importance. At the same time it is surprising to note the extent to which, in political matters, our 'practical Englishmen' are dominated by phrases. If we were to agree to a treaty of arbitration, a very large number of people in England would believe that the Germans had put off their desire for conquest and had become peaceable individuals. In exchange we could afford to build a few more battleships, especially if they were not given too much publicity."

I have quoted these opinions of experienced observers since they illustrate what are, in fact, the main faults of British statesmen in their handling of international problems. There is considerable ignorance, not so much of foreign conditions, as of foreign psychology; there is unbounded optimism; there is a dislike of facing unpleasant possibilities in advance; and there is a tendency to welcome transactions and agreements which, while they have no real validity, are calculated to appeal to the sentiment of the British public and their love of comforting phrases.

The British diplomatist inevitably reflects the merits and the defects of his political masters. I have already indicated that the Foreign Office and the Cabinet are apt to prefer their optimistic to their pessimistic ambassadors, and to regard those who warn them of coming dangers or disasters as "slightly unbalanced," "neurotic" or "unsound." An ambassador who has spent his life in the foreign service, and who has come to realize that the standards and mentality of foreigners are not always those of the English gentleman, is frequently appalled by the almost boyish serenity of Cabinet Ministers. If he be a man of great integrity and will-power he will gladly undergo the unpopularity which assails the prophet of woe, and assume the rôle of a Cassandra. But if he be a man of lesser character, he is tempted to reflect, and even to minister to, the serenity of his rulers; great damage may be done thereby to British foreign policy.

The British diplomatist, again, is rightly impressed by the supreme importance of avoiding any indiscretion, any intemperate word or action, which may place his government in an embarrassing position. Yet, as he becomes older, and the possibility of an ambassador's pension begins to glimmer before his eyes, he tends to reflect that a false step is a more terrible thing than no step at all and that, whereas an ill-judged action produces immediate chastisement, inactivity (if I may misquote Wordsworth) is:

> "permanent, obscure and dark
> And has the nature of Infinity."

In such circumstances the fine tradition of caution which animates the British foreign service declines into timidity.

Yet if British diplomacy reflects the failings of British policy—and is therefore apt to become all too optimistic, confused, non-committal, irrational and elastic—it also reflects its merits. The good British diplomatist is tolerant and fair; he acquires a fine balance between imagination and reason, between idealism and realism; he is reliable and scrupulously precise; he possesses dignity without self-importance, demeanour without mannerisms, poise without stolidity; he can display resolution as well as flexibility, and can combine gentleness with courage; he never boasts; he knows that impatience is as dangerous as ill-temper and that intellectual brilliance is not a diplomatic quality; he knows above all that it is his duty to interpret the policy of his government with loyalty and common sense and that the foundation of good diplomacy is the same as the foundation of good business—namely credit, confidence, consideration and compromise.

V

I have devoted this space to the discussion of the British type of diplomacy, not merely because it is the type of which I have had intimate and continuous knowledge all my life, but because I believe, in all sincerity, that it is on the whole the type which is most conducive to the maintenance of peaceful relations. I shall now pass to other types, and shall begin with the German type.

The German theory of policy, and therefore of diplomacy, is, as I have said before, a "heroic" or "warrior" conception and as such widely different from the mercantile or shop-keeper conception of the British. It also displays remarkable continuity.

It would be beyond the range of this monograph to examine the causes which have produced the type of mind which one can recognize as the distinctively German type of mind. Underneath all the solid and magnificent virtues of the German race there lies a layer of nervous uncertainty. This uncertainty (which has been defined by Friedrich Sieburg as " spiritual homelessness ") is due to a lack of any sharp geographical, racial or historical definition or outline. It all began when Augustus withdrew the Roman *limes* from the Elbe to the Danube, thus dividing the Germanies into the civilized and the barbarian. This disruption was later emphasized by the Reformation and the feeling that northern Germany was no more than a colony of the Holy Roman Empire. " We are," writes Sieburg, " shifting sand, yet in every grain there inheres the longing to combine with the rest into solid, durable stone." It is this desire to find some real focus, some centre of gravity, which has impelled the Germans to regard the conception of " unity," as expressed by the State, as something mystical and almost religious. It has also led them to find in physical unity, and therefore in physical power, that sense of solidarity which they lack as individuals.

The whole of modern German political theory from Fichte, via Hegel and Stewart Chamberlain, to Hitler is coloured by this emphasis upon some mystic union. The old thirteenth-century ideals of the Teutonic Order of the German Knights were inherited by Prussia who came to represent the ideal of German force, her pride of race, her yearning for political dominion. Fichte's original conception of the Germans as some "primordial people" (*Urvolk*) became linked with the later conceptions of "blood and iron," "blood and soil," and "blood and race." Fichte declared that "between States there is neither law nor right unless it be the right of the strongest." Hegel defined war as "eternal and moral." Thus German *Kultur* (which we most inaccurately translate as "culture") came to represent a general theory of mastery, of effort constantly renewed, of some mystical union between the German people and the elemental forces of nature.

German policy has been deeply affected by this philosophy. It is inspired by the ideal that German Kultur is some virile but inspired force which in the interests of humanity should impose itself upon the world. This ideal is essentially mystic. "Germany," writes Sieburg, "is a destiny, not a way of life." To that destiny the German individual citizen is prepared to sacrifice his mind, his independence, if necessary his life. "What distinguishes us," writes Sieburg again, "from other nations is the bounds we set to the instinct of self-preservation." In every German there is an element of suicidal mania.

The practical interpretation of this ideal assumes several forms. In so far as foreign policy and diplomacy are concerned it expresses itself in two ways. On the one hand there is the belief that force, or the threat of force, are the main instruments of negotiation. And on the other hand there is the theory that the "*raison d'état*," or needs of the State, take precedence over all individual religions or philosophies.

German policy, therefore, is essentially "*Machtpolitik*" or "Power policy." Her diplomacy, as I have indicated before, reflects this warrior or military conception. It seems to them more important to inspire fear than to beget confidence; and when, as invariably happens, the frightened nations combine to protect themselves, the Germans complain of "*Einkreisung*" or "encirclement," wholly ignoring the fact that it is their own methods and menaces which have produced this reaction.

A characteristic symptom of the warrior conception of policy is what Professor Mowat has called "sudden diplomacy." Of all forms of diplomacy that assuredly is the most dangerous. Its theoretical basis is that it demonstrates strength, causes perturbation, and thereby increases opportunity for pressure. Its practical justification is that it provides the negotiator with "something in hand." The classic instance of sudden diplomacy is Count Aerenthal's seizure of Bosnia Herzegovina in 1908. It was eminently successful at the moment, but it left behind it the legacy of fear and of resentment which led eventually to the destruction of the Austro-Hungarian Empire. Other instances of this sudden or surprise diplomacy have occurred in more recent years. It is a conception of negotiation which is often resorted to by German diplomatists. It is essentially a military conception.

It might be argued that the art of negotiation, which is a civilian art, can find but small place in a state-theory so largely dominated by military ideas. True it is that German foreign policy has always tended to be subsidiary to "*Machtpolitik*" and that the General Staff often exercise greater influence upon policy than do the Foreign Office. True it is also that the German belief in the leadership principle, and their tendency to concentrate power in the hands of a single individual, has prevented the German foreign service from acquiring the same corporate consciousness, technique or independence as its British counterpart. Yet the fact remains that, in spite of these disadvantages, the German diplomatic and consular service are fine professions, staffed by most efficient and honourable men. The German Ambassadors before the war were usually drawn from the profession itself and had thus acquired a clearer sense of the common interests of Europe, and a more sensitive understanding of foreign psychology, than was possessed by the bureaucrats in Berlin. It is almost tragic to read the despatches and memoirs of these diplomatists and to observe how frequently their councils were ignored or misinterpreted or dismissed by the Emperor or his Chancellors.

Nor can it be said that the discipline and loyalty of the German foreign service can be compared with the standards expected from the diplomatist of other countries. It was Bismarck who first introduced the system of appointing as secretaries to German Embassies abroad agents of his own choosing, whose function was to spy upon their Ambassador. This system was brought to a fine art by Fritz von Holstein who, during his long period of influence in the Wilhelmstrasse, entangled the whole German foreign service in a spider's web of suspicion, jealousy and intrigue. It was largely owing to the influence of that almost demented bureaucrat that the high principles and wise judgment of the elder German diplomatists were so often rendered ineffective. And even after Holstein's disappearance, Prince Lichnowsky complained that his efforts to warn his government of the probable effects of their policy in 1914 were counteracted by other secret reports sent to Berlin by members of his own staff.

It might thus be said that German diplomatists have never been given a fair chance. Their moderation has been interpreted in Berlin as a sign of weakness or timidity; their counsels of prudence have been dismissed as un-German; their rectitude has been regarded with suspicion. It is not surprising that so many of their finer diplomatists should have retired in embittered disdain.

VI

French policy has, for the last sixty years, been governed almost exclusively by fear of her eastern neighbour and is thus more consistent than that of any other Great Power. The eyes of all French diplomatists remain eternally fixed on the "blue line of the Vosges," and their whole policy is directed towards defending themselves against the German menace. This constant preoccupation is apt to render French policy tense, rigid and inelastic.

The French diplomatic service ought to be the best in the world. It possesses a long tradition and the recent example of such ideal diplomatists as the two Cambons, Jusserand, Barrère, and Berthelot. It is staffed by men of remarkable intelligence, wide experience and great social charm. The French combine with acuteness of observation a special gift of lucid persuasiveness. They are honourable and precise. Yet they lack tolerance. So convinced is the average Frenchman of his own intellectual pre-eminence, so conscious is he of the superiority of his own culture, that he finds it difficult at times to conceal his impatience with the barbarians who inhabit other countries. This causes offence.

The concentration, again, of the French mind upon a particular line of policy prevents them on occasions from observing events which lie outside their immediate and intense focus. All diplomatists are bound to place the interests of their own countries in the forefront of their consciousness: yet for the French, the interests of France loom so exclusively that the forefront is apt to become blocked. Moreover, their passion for logic, the legal temper of their minds, their extreme realism, their distrust of all political emotion, often blind them to the motives, the feelings and often the thoughts of other nations. Their superb intellectual integrity tempts them to regard as insincere the confused fumblings of less lucid minds and to feel irritated, dry contempt, when what is necessary is a little lucubrating indulgence. It thus occurs that French diplomacy, with all its magnificent equipment and its fine principles, is often ineffective. Nor do the professional politicians always allow to the professional diplomatists that scope which is their due.

The rigidity of French diplomacy stands in striking contrast to the mobile diplomacy of the Italians. The Italian system is derived from the traditions of the Italian States of the Renaissance and is based neither on the sound business concept, nor on power-policy, nor on the logical attainment of certain ends. It is more than opportunist, it is based upon incessant manœuvre.

The aim of Italy's foreign policy is to acquire by negotiation an importance greater than can be supplied by her own physical strength. It is thus the antithesis of the German system, since instead of basing diplomacy on power she bases power on diplomacy. It is the antithesis of the French system, since instead of striving to secure permanent allies against a permanent enemy, she regards her allies and her enemies as interchangeable. It is the antithesis of the British system, since it is not durable credit that she seeks for, but immediate advantage. Her conception, moreover, of the Balance of Power is not identical with the British conception; for whereas in Great Britain that doctrine is interpreted as opposition to any country who may seek to dominate Europe, in Italy it is desired as a balance of such equipoise that her own weight can tilt the scale.

Italian diplomatists make a speciality of the art of negotiation. Their usual method is first to create bad relations with the country with whom they wish to negotiate and then to offer "good relations." Before entering upon such negotiations they are careful to provide themselves with three bargaining counters. The first of these is a sense of grievance and hostility which are artificially provoked among the Italian people. The second is some form of nuisance-value against the country with which Italy is about to negotiate. And the third is a claim for some concession which Italy does not expect to obtain, or really desires, but the abandonment of which will oblige the other country to pay some compensation. As the negotiations proceed, these counters are added to by others. And, if the negotiations show signs of becoming difficult, a hint is given that similar negotiations will be opened elsewhere. Occasionally concurrent negotiations are undertaken with two opposing sides. Thus in 1914–16 Italy simultaneously negotiated with her allies and with their enemies regarding the concessions which the former would pay for her neutrality, and the latter for her assistance. The latter were in the position to offer a higher price.

Italy's diplomacy, ingenious though it be, is not perhaps a fair sample of the art of negotiation. She combines, on the one hand, the ambitions and the pretensions of a Great Power with, on the other, the methods of a Small Power. Her policy is thus not volatile only but essentially transitional. Modern Italy has already produced diplomatists, such as Sforza and Grandi, who have rightly won general esteem. It is confidently to be expected that now that Italy is becoming a Great Power, in fact as well as in name, her diplomacy will become more stable and more dignified.

CHAPTER VII

RECENT CHANGES IN DIPLOMATIC PRACTICE

Diplomacy by Conference—Its popularity now on the decline—Its advantages and defects—The demand for increased democratic control—Diplomacy and commercial interests—The creation of the Commercial Diplomatic Service—The "Press Attaché" and his functions—The dangers of propaganda—The League of Nations—Its secretariat—The British Commonwealth of Nations as a new experiment in international co-operation

I HAVE now examined the origin and development of diplomatic theory and practice ; I have considered the faults and virtues both of the old and the new diplomacy ; and I have contrasted the qualities of the ideal diplomatist with certain defects imposed upon this admirable profession by different types of policy. I propose in the present chapter to discuss the main innovations introduced into diplomatic practice by such post-war developments as the movement towards greater democratic control, the increasing importance of economics and finance, the inventions of modern science, and a more enlightened (although still restricted) conception of the community of international interests.

It was felt after the War of 1914–18 that diplomatic intercourse would henceforward be conducted almost entirely by round-table conferences. In a valuable address which he delivered to the Royal Institute of International Affairs on November 2, 1920, Sir Maurice Hankey, who had himself attended 488 International Meetings since 1914, expressed the considered opinion that "It can hardly be doubted that diplomacy by conference has come to stay."

It had been found during the war that agreement between the several Allied Governments on matters of immediate importance could not rapidly be secured by the ordinary methods of diplomatic communication. It became essential that at regular intervals the Prime Ministers or experts of the several Powers should meet round a table and discuss the urgent problems of strategy and policy which the joint conduct of the war imposed. There were in addition innumerable technical problems, such as food and transport, in regard to which all the Allies were faced by common dangers and common necessities. They were obliged to pool their resources and to agree upon the priority of their respective needs. A whole network of inter-allied committees, or permanent conferences, was therefore created. These ranged from great organizations such as the Allied Council on War Purchases and Finance, the Commission Internationale de Ravitaillement, the Allied Food Council, and the Allied Maritime Transport Council, to smaller committees of experts dealing with such supplies as coal, nitrates, cotton, petroleum and timber. These several councils and committees were co-ordinated into a definite pattern in the shape of a pyramid, of which the base was represented by the several sub-committees on specific supplies, and of which the apex culminated in the Supreme War Council of the Allied and Associated Powers.

In his valuable history of the development and functions of the Allied Maritime Transport Council, entitled *Allied Shipping Control*, Sir Arthur Salter shows how these international committees became in course of time something more than a mere war-time machinery of co-ordination. They constituted a fundamental innovation in what until then had been the usual practice of international negotiation. In the place of a national policy expressing itself by competitive and conflicting diplomacy, you had a common international interest imposing the need of international co-operation. Nor was this the only difference. Instead of national policy trying to impose itself from above upon the facts of a situation you had a system by which the facts imposed themselves upon a policy. It was found that a body of international experts, when dealing under the pressure of a common danger with very concrete facts, acquired a more continuous standard of mutual confidence and co-operation than professional diplomatists had ever managed to achieve. And it was hoped by many of us that this new experiment in conducting diplomacy from below upwards might in fact prove a valuable innovation in international practice.

To a certain extent these hopes were realized in the Secretariat of the League of Nations, a body which acquired and still maintains the highest standards of efficiency and co-operation. Yet when once the common danger had been removed, the great War Councils of the Allies shared the fate of the old Amphictyonic Councils—disintegration set in.

The advantages of diplomacy by conference are self-evident. It enables those who are responsible for framing policy to conduct negotiation. Immense time is saved by this method and greater flexibility is acquired. In the course of frequent meetings the several Prime Ministers come to know, and sometimes even to trust, each other. "Real intimacy," writes Sir Maurice Hankey, "and friendship materially contribute to the success of diplomacy by conference by rendering possible absolute frankness of discussion."

This is true. Yet it is possible that, in place of friendship, antipathy may result from such frequent contacts. The personal relations between

Lord Curzon, for instance, and M. Poincaré did not assist negotiation. Even friendship may lead (as at the Thoiry luncheon-party between Briand and Stresemann) to some impulsive settlement which has thereafter to be repudiated. The dangers of imprecision, misunderstanding, leakage and indiscretion are much increased. And rapidity of discussion is not, in times of peace, invariably an advantage.

Of recent years, and as a result of successive discomfitures, the popularity of diplomacy by conference has, in Great Britain at least, sensibly declined. Berchtesgaden and Munich have confirmed this distaste. The British public have always had an instinctive dislike of these international gatherings as was shown by their suspicion of the Congress system which the Emperor Alexander and Metternich tried to perpetuate after the Napoleonic wars. And it was generally felt that the autumn sessions of the League of Nations Assembly provided all the contacts which should normally be necessary, without investing these meetings of ministers with that atmosphere of exaggerated public expectancy which is the bane of all special or sensational conferences.

Obviously, however, there are occasions when a conference becomes essential. Yet, if it is to succeed, the ground must be most carefully prepared beforehand. No conference should ever be attempted until its scope and programme have been agreed to by all the participants and until, through the ordinary diplomatic channels, it has been ascertained that the views of the negotiating parties are not hopelessly at variance. The success of the London Conference on Reparations, which produced what was known as " The Dawes Plan," was due to careful preliminary arrangements arrived at between Ramsay MacDonald and M. Herriot at Chequers. The failure of the Naval Disarmament Conference at Geneva in 1926 and the even more tragic failure of the World Economic Conference of 1933, can be ascribed almost wholly to lack of the necessary preliminary soundings between London and Washington. This golden rule is not sufficiently understood by politicians.

II

To-day, therefore, it could scarcely be said that diplomacy by conference has " come to stay." In 1920 it certainly appeared as if the lessons in co-operation which the war had taught to Europe would produce something like a fundamental change in diplomatic practice. To-day the tide is setting against the new system and towards a return to diplomacy by professional experts acting under written instructions. Yet, although this particular innovation has for the moment declined in popularity, there are other changes in diplomatic practice and functions which are likely to survive and to develop.

It is probable, for instance, that in countries which still enjoy representative institutions, there will be an increased demand for democratic control over both policy and negotiation. This demand is frequently made without full knowledge of the working of the constitution and is based, as I have said, upon some confusion between "policy" and "negotiation." Yet the demand is general and is likely to increase in volume as a result of the Czechoslovak crisis of August–September 1938.

Even those who are aware of the very effective control which can be exercised by the legislature owing to its power to refuse to ratify treaties, are apt to contend that there should exist some additional, and more continuous, form of parliamentary supervision over the conduct of foreign policy by a government and its servants. In Great Britain this movement has in the past concentrated upon the demand for a Foreign Affairs Committee of the House of Commons, endowed with the same privileges and prestige as the Foreign Relations Committee in the United States, or the analogous Parliamentary Committee in France.

The advantages of such committees are that they enable the Foreign Secretary accurately to gauge parliamentary opinion, while they provide Parliament with a safety-valve for such criticism and suggestion as would be impossible in a public debate. The disadvantages are that they impose extra labour on the Foreign Secretary; that they often emphasize difficulties and disagreements which might be solved by the passage of silent time; that they introduce an element of party controversy into the conduct of international affairs; that they constitute a channel through which financial and commercial interests might seek unduly to influence policy; and that, invariably and irremediably, they lead to serious indiscretions and disclosures.

The parties which support the National Government in Great Britain have of recent years experimented with a purely unofficial Foreign Affairs Committee to which opposition members are not admitted. This Committee exists ostensibly for the private discussion of foreign problems and is precluded by its own rules either from testing opinion by a vote or from addressing resolutions to the Government. It is certainly of great value in that it allows members to exchange views, to acquire information, and to hear from time to time confidential statements from the Foreign Secretary. It also enables the whips to gauge the opinion of the party. Yet it is not an official or elected body, and it possesses no power to impose a majority view upon the government of the day.

III

A further, and more compelling, cause of change in diplomatic practice is the increased importance of commerce. In one sense this is no new development. It could be contended in fact that diplomacy as an organized profession owed as much to commercial interests as to political interests. It would be possible to argue that the main impulse which transformed the old amateur diplomacy into a specialized service, was the impulse of trade. The Venetian diplomatic service, which undoubtedly laid the foundations of professional diplomacy, was in its origin a commercial machinery. Our own diplomatic representatives in the Near and the Far East had commercial origins. Organizations such as the Levant Company maintained at their expense and with the moral support of the Government, envoys who were half official and half mercantile. These agents were never certain whether their main allegiance was owed to their own Board of Directors or to the Government.

This dual allegiance was abolished when the Ambassador or Minister became the personal representative of his Sovereign. So anxious became these plenipotentiaries to disclaim any connection with the old "Company Agent" that, as the years progressed, they assumed that any connection with commerce implied a lowering of their own status from sovereign representatives to commercial travellers. It is this curve of development from trade to politics and then back to trade which explains the distaste which those who fell within the middle period felt for commercial activities.

Thus, during the early nineteenth century, a British diplomatist would have felt sullied were he to engage in pushing the material requirements of his nationals. He was prepared, and to any lengths, to protect and defend their personal liberty. He was not expected, or prepared, to assist them in making commercial profits.

It was the Germans who first realized the utility of combining political with commercial advantages. The Americans followed. In the days of the old diplomacy one political advantage was bargained against another political advantage: by the middle of the nineteenth century, commercial advantages were also thrown into the balance. The concession-hunter appeared. One of the first symptoms of this alteration in the incidence of political interest was the competition which arose in Turkey and China between rival railway interests. It was this competition which convinced the chancelleries of Europe that there was some connection between capitalist exploitation and political influence.

The professional diplomatist of the old school fought for long against this commercial connection. His idea was that in any case the political relations between different countries were complicated enough without adding to their complexity by official commercial rivalry. He had a prejudice against all concession-hunters as against economic imperialism, he believed in *laisser faire*, and he was conscious that trade and finance were subjects of which he had but slight experience. Yet he was fighting a losing battle and by the last three decades of the nineteenth century the principle had become established that the functions of the foreign service comprised, not only the protection, but also the furtherance of private commercial interests.

In Great Britain a Commercial Department of the Foreign Office was established in 1866 and thoroughly reorganized in 1872. A Commercial Attaché was appointed to the Paris Embassy in 1880 and to St. Petersburg in 1887. The business world continued to complain that the British diplomatic, consular and commercial officials did not display the same activity on behalf of their traders as was shown by the German and the American services. The information supplied by the consular reports, or in reply to inquiries from Chambers of Commerce, was, they said, inadequate and sometimes misleading; the relations between embassies or legations and the local commercial community were distant and cold; and, although they could look to their diplomatic representatives for protection against flagrant injustice, they were not accorded, as their German and American rivals were accorded, sufficiently energetic support in marketing their wares. Successive committees were appointed to examine these grievances and with useful results. In 1903 the Consular Service was almost completely reorganized and more commercial attachés were appointed. A problem of co-ordination arose owing to the dual functions of the Commercial Intelligence Department of the Board of Trade and the Commercial Department of the Foreign Office. It was not until after the war that this problem was solved by the creation of the Department of Overseas Trade and by placing the commercial attachés upon an entirely new basis both as regards status and recruitment. In place of the old system a regular commercial diplomatic service was established, the officers of which were given titles and status analogous to those of the political branch and were accorded adequate provision for offices, clerical assistance and entertainment.

There is now every prospect that this new commercial service will develop its own traditions and its own identity. It is able to supply the business community with expert and detailed information and with most effective assistance; and it is warmly welcomed by the diplomatic service itself as ridding them of an embarrassing, and sometimes uncongenial, task to which they knew themselves to be unfitted.

Another change in the old conventions of diplomatic procedure has been caused by the increasing importance of such international problems as currency and finance. The old diplomatic convention was that all negotiations must be carried out between the head of a mission and the Foreign Office of the country to which he was accredited; and it would have been regarded as a serious breach of etiquette were a member of a foreign mission to hold converse with any other department. This convention was shattered by the war. Mr. Lloyd George, when he was Chancellor of the Exchequer, entered into direct negotiations with the French Minister of Finance, and when later he became Minister of Munitions his relations with M. Albert Thomas were continuous and close. Moreover, it was found that many of these important matters of controversy and discussion required technical knowledge of the problems that they covered, and that the ordinary diplomatist did not possess that specialized knowledge of currency or finance which would enable him to negotiate upon such subjects. The excellent practice thus arose of entrusting such negotiations to Treasury experts and of maintaining, as financial attachés to certain embassies, men who had spent their lives in the study of these particular problems.

IV

The increasing importance and power of the Press has also led to the appointment, to the major embassies abroad, of an official who is known as a "Press Attaché." The functions of this official are numerous and diverse. He is expected to read, digest and translate the articles published in the local journals. He interviews British and other Press correspondents and tries to secure that the views of his government obtain adequate publicity. And he is able to establish contacts with local journalists who provide valuable information.

He has a further utility. For whereas ambassadors and their staffs are constantly shifting from capital to capital, the Press Attaché is usually retained in the same post for a period of several years. This comparative permanence of tenure enables him to acquire great knowledge of local politics and personalities. An ambassador, especially in some continental countries, where political passions run high, finds it difficult to get to know those politicians who are opposed to the government in power. It was delicate, if not impossible, for instance, for a British Ambassador in Tsarist Russia to establish any contact with Russian Liberals of the type of Miliukoff or Lwoff. A Press Attaché is able to maintain such contacts without causing offence. His position can thus be one of great usefulness and considerable importance, and the system should be extended to every important mission.

A new and serious problem of modern diplomacy is the problem of propaganda. In the days of the old diplomacy it would have been regarded as an act of unthinkable vulgarity to appeal to the common people upon any issue of international policy. It was Canning, in 1826, who first recognized the efficacy of what he called " the fatal artillery of popular excitation." Prince Metternich did not share this view, although it caused him much disquiet. He accused Canning of seeking to acquire popularity—" a pretension that is misplaced in a statesman."

If Canning was the first British statesman deliberately to recognize public opinion as an instrument of policy, he was careful to lay down the condition that such opinion must be founded upon truth and justice. Those continental statesmen who adopted his theory in the later half of the nineteenth century dispensed with this condition. Bismarck and his imitators were accustomed to invent incidents or to distort facts in order to inflame public opinion upon some specific issue. Yet, although Bismarck, and even Bülow, did not hesitate to inspire untruthfulness in others, they refrained from telling demonstrable lies themselves. In fact, until the war of 1914–18 came to degrade all international standards, it was still considered unfitting and unwise for a statesman to make public pronouncements to his own people which public opinion in other countries would know to be totally untrue.

The war abolished all such delicacies of conscience. Even the British (who are a truthful race) gradually acquired a taste for propaganda, and proved that they also could tell deliberate lies. British war propaganda was perhaps neither so brilliant as Adolf Hitler assures us, nor as efficacious as Mr. Squires contends; but by the last years of the war it had become a highly organized system and certainly provided a formidable weapon of popular excitation.

Since then, the invention of the wireless has given a vast impetus to propaganda as a method of policy. Herr Hitler has himself devoted many years of study to the problem and has embodied his conclusions in the earlier sections of "*Mein Kampf.*" He affirms the axiom that the masses are more easily stirred by the human voice than by any other form of communication. Yet propaganda by wireless must, if it is to be successful, recognize certain principles. In the first place, so Herr Hitler assures us, it must aim at the lowest types of mind. It must avoid all intellectual considerations and must seek to arouse the emotions only. Its method must be one of "inspiring fanaticism and occasionally hysteria." There must never be any suggestion that there can be something to be said for the other side. There must be no subtleties or reservations but "only a positive and a negative, love and hatred, right and wrong, truth and lies, never any half and half." And above all, so Hitler tells us, the lies must be enormous; it is no use, in his opinion, telling little lies; a propaganda lie must be of such gigantic proportions that listeners will never suspect that it could be invented.

It is evident that this system of propaganda by wireless can in certain circumstances do immense damage to international relations. Thus the incessant anti-British propaganda which Signor Mussolini broadcast from the Bari station in Arabic was, had the British Government so chosen to take it, a definitely unfriendly act. Its suppression became one of the main objects of the Anglo-Italian agreement. And it is evident that if nations are to address each other in terms which are deliberately intended to arouse hysteria among the lowest types of the population, the old courtesies of diplomatic intercourse will wear a trifle thin.

A further danger of propaganda is that those who use it are liable to become its victims. Thus, when in 1919 Signor Orlando, in order to impress President Wilson with the depth of Italian popular feeling regarding Fiume, organized an intense propaganda in his own country, he found that such violent emotions had been aroused that it had become impossible for him to accept a reasonable solution. An even sadder instance is that provided by the Nazi propaganda over the Sudeten Germans; passions were unleashed which became uncontrollable and Herr Hitler found himself in a position where even a diplomatic triumph would have been regarded as a defeat.

It is difficult to suggest by what means diplomacy can mitigate the dangers of this terrible invention. International agreements on the subject are evaded or ignored; counter-propaganda only intensifies the conflict. The most that can be hoped is that the very virulence of the method, the actual iteration of demonstrable untruths, may in the end defeat its own purpose. And that the best antidote to the hysterical school of broadcasters is a policy of truth, under-statement and calm.

It is difficult to state with any accuracy what sums are expended by the several governments upon their propaganda services. It is estimated that Germany spends some £4,000,000 to £6,000,000 annually on foreign propaganda. France spends some £1,200,000 and Italy the equivalent of nearly £1,000,000. In Great Britain no sums are allocated for propaganda as such, although grants are given to the British Council as follows :

1935 . .	£5,000
1936 . .	£15,000
1937 . .	£60,000
1938 . .	£100,000 with a possible addition of £40,000

The British Council is an officially created and subsidized body the purpose of which is to make British life and thought more widely known abroad, to encourage the study of the English language, and to render available abroad current British contributions to literature, science or the fine arts. Apart from the sums allocated to the British Council no British funds are spent on propaganda.

V

Of all the innovations which affected diplomacy since the war, the most important is the League of Nations. It is not my purpose to examine the origins of the League idea, or to consider what were the causes and mistakes which have rendered it, at moments of trial, inadequate to its own purposes. It is easy to say that it is based upon a conception of international unselfishness which, were it a true conception, would render any league unnecessary. It is easy to say that the League became impossible so soon as any one Great Power either left or defied it; that its identification with the maintenance of the Peace Treaties destroyed from the outset its moral authority; that its conduct at the time of the Silesian settlement or the Corfu incident should have warned all but sentimentalists that it was essentially opportunist and timid; and that the instinct of self-preservation which is at the root of all policy must deter any country from risking an unsuccessful war for the sake of another. Such criticism is self-evident; but it is not final. The League idea is certain, unless force triumphs in Europe, to emerge again.

Meanwhile, the continued existence of the League since 1920 has modified in some important respects the older practices of diplomacy. Apart from the fundamental conception of an organization of mutual insurance against war; apart from the surrender of national sovereignty which a strict adherence to the Covenant would imply; the League represents an innovation in all previous attempts at international co-operation, and for three main reasons. In the first place it is based upon a covenant or body of rules and principles. In the second place it holds annual meetings in a definite locality and at a definite time. And in the third place it possesses a permanent secretariat of trained international experts.

This third innovation, as I have indicated above, is not the least in importance. Men and women of different nationalities are collaborating constantly together for certain common aims; they have no desire to impose any national doctrine or to serve any national interest; their ambition is to ascertain the truth about the political and economic factors which make for unrest; and in pursuing that ambition they acquire a truly international spirit and are able to transfer something of that spirit to the politicians who attend the Councils and Assemblies.

Even if it could be argued that the League has ceased to be a determining factor in political appeasement, it could not be denied that its economic and social activities are of the greatest importance. It is to be hoped that, if the world recovers its sanity, it will be through such organizations that it will come to realize again that co-operation is a better thing than conflict.

A further, and so far more successful, experiment in international co-operation is the British Commonwealth of Nations. The independent status acquired by the British Dominions was emphasized by their direct representation at the Paris Conference and by their signature, as separate countries, of the treaties of peace. The Imperial Conference of 1926 defined the position of the Dominions in the following terms:

"They are autonomous Communities within the British Empire, equal in status, in no way subordinate one to another in any aspect of their domestic or external affairs, though united by a common allegiance to the Crown, and freely associated as members of the British Commonwealth of Nations."

This principle was given legislative sanction by the Statute of Westminster of December 11, 1931.

The British Commonwealth of Nations is a completely new experiment in the adjustment of the relations between independent States. No previous league, federation, or coalition has in this way dispensed with all written constitutions or treaties of alliance. It is evident that so fundamental a departure from all previous precedent must raise many new problems, not the least of which are those connected with the framing and conduct of foreign policy.

Co-ordination between the several members of the Commonwealth is secured by three main methods. In the first place a conference of all the members is held every four years. In the second place each member may be represented in the capital of each other member by a High Commissioner. And in the third place the governments of the several Dominions may, if they so desire, receive full information from the British Government regarding current issues in foreign affairs or on questions which are of common interest to all the members of the Commonwealth.

The Dominions may, if they wish, maintain diplomatic representatives of their own in foreign capitals with the rank of envoys extraordinary and ministers plenipotentiary. Thus Canada has her own envoys in Paris, Washington and Tokyo; South Africa in Rome, Washington and The Hague; and Eire in France, Germany, the United States and at the Vatican. Conversely the French maintain legations in Canada and Eire; the United States in Canada, South Africa and Eire, and so on.

These Dominion Legations report direct to their own governments and have no special connection with the British Embassies in the capitals where they exist. Although the Dominion governments have not as yet established regular Foreign Offices yet a section of the Prime Minister's offices is staffed, in Australia and Canada at least, by specialists in foreign affairs. In 1935 Australia created a special 'Department of External Affairs' which has now a staff of seventeen. A similar development is taking place in Canada.

This glorious experiment is not, as yet, fully understood by foreign diplomatists. They imagine that members of the British Commonwealth are bound by some secret compact to support each other in all international negotiations, and they are apt to resent the fact that the British Government should (as they imagine) be able to control the votes of her Dominions at any international conference. This assumption is incorrect. There is nothing which need prevent a Dominion government from taking a wholly independent line in foreign policy. The only stipulation which exists is that passed by the 1923 Imperial Conference under which members of the Commonwealth are asked not to negotiate treaties with foreign governments "without due consideration of its possible effect upon other parts of the Empire, or on the Empire as a whole."

So loose a confederation would certainly crumble were it not united by strong ties of sentiment and by the fact that, whereas the interests and ambitions of the several members seldom come into acute conflict, their needs of security and self-preservation hold them together.

CHAPTER VIII

POINTS OF DIPLOMATIC PROCEDURE

Precedence among States—Instances of the struggle for precedence—Great and Small Powers—The modern practice of raising the status of Legations into Embassies—Precedence of ambassadors in various countries—The appointment of an envoy—How he is selected—The "agrément"—The arrival of an envoy—He presents his letters—Differences in ceremonial—The recall of an envoy—The Chauvelin case—The case of M. de St. Quentin—The recognition of insurgents and revolutionaries—Rupture of diplomatic relations—How an envoy reports to his own government—His communications with the government to which he is accredited—The functions of an envoy—Subjects with which he deals—Social activities—Procedure at conferences and congresses

HAVING discussed the various types of diplomatic theory and practice and having considered the changes which have been introduced since the war, I now propose to examine certain rules of procedure which have survived the vicissitudes of the last hundred years and which are still generally recognized by civilized governments as being those most conducive to orderly diplomatic intercourse.

I have already referred to the question of precedence and have drawn attention to the fact that it was many centuries before the nations of the world came to agree upon this vexed problem. Immense importance was attached by the old diplomacy to the precedence, or order of importance, of the several States.

In the old days the Pope claimed the right to decide in what order the nations of the world should be listed, and there exists a memorandum of 1504 in which this order is laid down. The Pope, not unnaturally, placed himself first among the monarchs of the earth. The Emperor came second and after him his heir-apparent, "The King of the Romans." Then followed the Kings of France, Spain, Aragon and Portugal. Great Britain came sixth on the list and the King of Denmark last. This papal class-list was not accepted without demur by the sovereigns concerned. It often happened that a French Ambassador had been instructed by his sovereign in no case to yield precedence to the Spanish Ambassador, whereas the latter had received exactly similar instructions. Undignified scenes took place at court functions; at a court ball in London in 1768, a scuffle took place between the French and Russian Ambassadors which terminated in a duel.

A classic example of these struggles for precedence is the case of the Spanish Ambassador's carriage in 1661. It was in those days the custom for foreign envoys to make their entry with a great apparatus of state. Their foreign colleagues were expected to send their gala coaches in order to add magnificence to the procession. Thus when, on September 30, 1661, a new Swedish envoy disembarked at the Tower wharf in London, both the Spanish and the French Ambassadors had sent their coaches to greet him. The Swedish envoy sanded, entered the royal coach which had been lent to meet him, and drove off. The French Ambassador's coachman edged his horses immediately behind the Swedish equipage, an action which was regarded by the coachman of the Spanish Ambassador as a direct insult to the King of Spain. A struggle ensued which (since each coach had been accompanied by some 150 armed men) assumed serious proportions. The French coachman was pulled from his box, two of the horses were hamstrung, and a postilion was killed. Louis XIV thereupon severed diplomatic relations with Spain, and threatened to declare war unless a full apology were given and the Spanish Ambassador in London were punished. The King of Spain, anxious to avoid hostilities, agreed to make the necessary apologies and reparation.

It was not only at official receptions that this conflict over precedence destroyed amity and interrupted business. Before any international conference there would be long, and occasionally fruitless, negotiations regarding the order in which the representatives of the several countries would sit at the conference table. Even when that point had been settled, a further difficulty arose as to the order in which they would append their signatures. A device was invented, called the "alternat," by which each representative signed his own copy of the treaty first; yet even this device provided for no regular order in which the other signatures should follow.

By Article 4 of the Règlement, laid down by the Congress of Vienna in 1815, it was agreed that diplomatic representatives should take rank according to the date of the official notification of their arrival. It also became established that plenipotentiaries at a conference should sign treaties in alphabetical order.

This put an end to the more acute controversies regarding precedence, but it left certain other points unsettled. The generally accepted idea was that only Great Powers could exchange ambassadors, whereas the diplomatic representatives despatched or received by the Small Powers (or, as they were tactfully called, "Powers with limited interests") should be of the rank of minister. Yet who is to say which power is "great" or "small"? At the Paris Conference of 1919 the five Great Powers of the United States, France, Great Britain, Italy and Japan styled themselves "The Principal Allied and Associated Powers," and assumed the right to form the main Council of the Conference to the exclusion of their smaller allies. Yet the empirical nature of such distinctions is shown by the variations in diplomatic rank between the several Powers which have taken place in recent years. At the beginning of Queen Victoria's reign Great Britain regarded only three Courts as worthy of receiving ambassadors, namely, Paris, St. Petersburg and Constantinople. Vienna was raised to an embassy in 1860, Berlin in 1862, Rome in 1876, Madrid in 1887, Washington in 1893, Tokio in 1905, Brussels in 1919, Rio in 1919, Lisbon in 1924, Buenos Aires in 1927, Warsaw in 1929, and Santiago in 1930. Since then, British Ambassadors have also been appointed to China, Egypt and Iraq. Many of these appointments have been made without regard to the power, status, or "precedence" of the countries concerned.

It is customary to deride these controversies over formal precedence and to assume that we to-day are wiser than our forefathers. Yet any student of diplomatic practice will agree that when they squabbled there was always some reasonable nucleus for their disputes. To-day we often speak of "national prestige" or "national honour": these important factors of power were, in the earlier centuries, symbolized by the order of precedence. It represented to them something analogous to what "insults to the flag" represented to later generations.

Even after the Congress of Vienna, this precedence question was not wholly solved. A country which enjoyed Legation rank was anxious to achieve Embassy rank, if only for purposes of national self-esteem. Thus when once the appointment of ambassadors to capitals other than those of admittedly Great Powers became a general, if invidious practice, it happened that other Powers who regarded themselves as the equals of those thus honoured became incensed. And so far from the appointment of ambassadors being a rare and exclusive privilege, a situation developed in which the denial of such appointment became an insult. As a result ambassador-currency became inflated.

Even in those countries who are generally regarded as "Great," the precedence of ambassadors is subject to variations. In monarchical countries the diplomatic body have precedence immediately below the members of the reigning family. In Great Britain Ambassadors are given precedence over anybody below the rank of Royal Highness. Ministers are listed after dukes but before marquesses. In France the Ambassadors and Ministers have to sit below the Presidents of the Senate and the Chamber of Deputies. In Washington the Vice-President has pride of place. In the South American Republics an attempt has often been made to seat foreign envoys below the members of the Cabinet. This has not met with success. Yet, in present days, these things are settled by rules which are known by all and tacitly admitted. It is improbable that even a totalitarian ambassador would to-day consider it desirable to organize a scene.

II

I now come to the actual procedure which governs the appointment of a diplomatic envoy from one State to another. I shall take as my example of the usual practice the system adopted in the British Foreign Service.

The head of some mission retires, or is transferred elsewhere, and it becomes necessary to choose his successor. In theory, this choice rests entirely with the Foreign Secretary, yet he will be guided in his selection by the advice of his permanent officials. In former days this advice was tendered by his own Private Secretary; more recently, it was found that this system was regarded as invidious, and a small appointments-committee of senior officials has been established for this purpose. If the post which has to be filled is of great importance the Foreign Secretary will consult with the Prime Minister or even the Cabinet as a whole. In the British service there is nothing to prevent the Secretary of State from appointing someone outside the professional ranks. Some of the most successful British Ambassadors (and notably Lord Bryce, Lord D'Abernon, Lord Crewe and Lord Derby) had never been members of the Diplomatic Service. The present tendency is only to make these outside appointments in exceptional circumstances.

Having decided on a suitable person, the Secretary of State then writes him a private letter offering the post. It is always possible that the incumbent may plead ill-health or domestic reasons and may ask to be excused. The British Foreign Office is considerate in such cases. If he accepts, the next step is to obtain the *agrément* of the country to which he is to be sent. It is customary to make private enquiries before asking officially whether a given individual is likely to prove a *persona grata*. The government to which the enquiry is addressed will, if in any doubt, consult their own embassy as to the character and antecedents of the person suggested. If the *agrément* is refused, some mortification will result, and the rejected envoy will be glad if he has had sufficient discretion not to inform his friends of the offer which had been made to him.

If the *agrément* is given, the incumbent of the post will return to London and make the necessary preparations for his departure. In former days an ambassador or minister proceeding to a new post was provided with written instructions, and many of these instructions were in the nature of important

State Papers. Now that the head of a mission abroad can ask for instructions at any moment this practice has lapsed. Such instructions as he receives will be conveyed in verbal interviews with the head of the department concerned and with the Secretary of State. There will also be available for him at the Foreign Office the annual reports of his predecessors, the reports upon local notabilities, and the reports upon the members of the diplomatic body in the capital to which he is being sent. A study of these reports will enable him, before leaving, to obtain a rough idea of the problems, personalities and colleagues with which and whom he will have to cope.

He will then notify the staff of his future mission of the date and hour of his arrival. The old ceremonies of a state entry have in modern diplomatic procedure been abandoned. In Persia, until quite recently, it was still the custom to greet a new minister at the frontier at a ceremonial reception or "*istiqbal*." Yet even this kindly function has now been abolished, and the modern practice is to defer all ceremony until the official audience at which the new ambassador or minister presents his credentials.

The ceremonial prescribed for such occasions differs in the several countries. In Spain, before the revolution, the ambassador and his staff were conducted from the embassy in a long file of gala coaches with all the panoply of a royal procession. On arriving at the Palace they were greeted by the court officials and led to the royal presence through tapestried corridors lined by halbadiers.

In Washington the procedure is less decorative. The Ambassador drives in his own car to the State Department, whence he is accompanied by the Secretary of State to the White House. They enter the Blue Room and the Secretary of State then disappears for the purpose of notifying the President that they have now arrived. The President then enters, accompanied by his Secretary. The Ambassador reads his address and the President replies. The proceedings are then terminated.

The speeches delivered on such occasions are of a purely formal character and it is considered a breach of etiquette to mention in them any subject of controversy which may exist between the two governments.

Having presented his letters of credence, the envoy is then regarded as well and truly accredited. His next duty is to call upon the members of the Cabinet and upon his diplomatic colleagues. It will be many days before he has completed these irksome duties and is able to settle down to his work.

III

The presentation of letters of credence at the outset of a mission is a more important, and more ceremonial, function than the presentation of letters of recall at its termination. It is, for instance, a quite usual practice that an ambassador should be transferred from one post to another without presenting such letters, and in that case they are delivered by his successor at the same time as he presents his own letters of credence.

Apart from the normal procedure which is followed when an envoy is either accredited or recalled, there are certain rules which apply to abnormal situations. Such a situation arose at the end of 1792 between Pitt and Chauvelin, the Minister of France. Chauvelin's letters of credence had been in the name of Louis XVI, and when that monarch was deposed on August 10 he remained in England, but was only recognized as the agent of a *de facto* government in Paris. He continued, however, to address Notes to the British Government in an official capacity and on December 31, 1792, Pitt instructed Lord Grenville to address to him a sharp reminder:

"I have received, Sir, from you a Note in which, styling yourself minister plenipotentiary of France, you communicate to me, as the King's Secretary of State, the instructions which you state to have yourself received from the executive council of the French Republic.

You are not ignorant, that since the unhappy

events of the 10th of August, the King has thought proper to suspend all official communications with France. You are yourself no otherwise accredited to the King, than in the name of His Most Christian Majesty. The proposition of receiving a minister accredited by any other authority or power in France, would be a new question, which, whenever it should occur, the King would have the right to decide according to the interests of his subjects, his own dignity and the regard which he owes to his allies, and to the general system of Europe.

I am therefore to inform you, Sir, in express and formal terms that I acknowledge you in no other public character than that of minister from His Most Christian Majesty, and that consequently you cannot be admitted to treat with the King's ministers in the quality, and under the form, stated in your Note."

When, three weeks later, Louis XVI was executed, M. Chauvelin was dismissed the country.

An analogous difficulty arises when a sovereign has assumed a title which is not recognized by other countries. Thus when the King of Italy was named Emperor of Ethiopia by Mussolini a situation of great diplomatic complexity was created. The former French Ambassador had already left Rome and his successor, M. de St. Quentin, had already been appointed. It was evident that the latter would not be received in Rome if he failed to bring with him proper letters of credence, yet in those letters the name and titles of the King of Italy would have to be set out in due form. If that superscription omitted the words "Emperor of Ethiopia," M. de St. Quentin would not have been granted an audience; if they contained them, it would mean that France had officially recognized the conquest of Abyssinia. For many months this problem proved insoluble, and France was until recently only represented at the Quirinal by a chargé d'affaires.

In the event of the death or abdication of a sovereign new credentials are necessary, but they are not usually presented with similar ceremonial. The death or retirement of a president does not affect the validity of letters of credence delivered either to or by his predecessor.

A far more complicated problem is raised when a régime to which an envoy has been accredited is overthrown by revolution. There is, as I have said, no general rule governing the recognition of governments established by revolutionaries or insurgents. The decision to recognize or not to recognize is determined by expediency, although the principle is generally followed that no revolutionary government is recognized until it has established some degree of orderly administration over a sufficiently wide area. The practice adopted by the

British Government in such cases has never been uniform. Sometimes recognition has been withheld for a long period. At other times *de facto* recognition has been given almost at once. Occasionally, recognition has been conditional, as when British recognition of the Portuguese Republic was made conditional upon confirmation of the new régime by a general election. And on occasions (such as the Greek plebiscite of 1924, or the 1930 revolution in the Argentine) full *de jure* recognition has been accorded immediately.

It is often necessary, none the less, to open contact with a revolutionary government and this is done by means of an accredited agent. Such agents do not deliver letters of credence, since that would imply recognition, but are provided with a Note signed by the Secretary of State and indicating that they are authorized to negotiate with the authorities upon a *de facto* basis.

Complicated, and even painful, as the opening of diplomatic relations may sometimes be, it is their rupture which causes the greatest anguish. The termination of a mission may be due to several causes, only some of which are agreeable. Thus, an envoy may make himself so objectionable to the government to which he is accredited that his recall is demanded. In that event he is generally allowed to proceed " on indefinite leave of absence." In extreme cases he is actually " handed his passports " or told to leave the country, as happened to Chauvelin and Bulwer. It may occur even that the State to which he has been accredited ceases suddenly to exist, as Austria ceased in 1938. It may be that war is declared. Or it may be that one government decides to " break off diplomatic relations." This latter expedient is by no means always a prelude to war and is often resorted to as a means of expressing profound moral indignation. Thus the British Minister was withdrawn from Belgrade after the assassination of King Alexander and Queen Draga, even as a similar diplomatic rupture occurred when Colonel Plastiras murdered M. Gounaris and his ministers in November 1922.

IV

Once an envoy has presented his letters of credence and paid his official calls he is said to have " assumed his functions." These functions fall, for the most part, under two headings; he reports to his own government and he negotiates with the government to which he has been accredited.

His reports to his own government will take different forms. There is in the first place the formal despatch, which is addressed to the Secretary of State, carries a serial number, and is signed by the head of the mission. These despatches are drafted in a prescribed form. They begin " Sir " (or " My Lord " if the Foreign Secretary be a peer) and they generally open with some phrase giving a reference to previous correspondence on the same subject. Despatches from a Foreign Secretary to an ambassador or minister abroad are also framed in a similar form. The words used in termination vary according to the rank of the person addressed. To an ambassador, the Secretary of State signs as follows:

I am, with great truth and respect,
Sir,
Your obedient servant,

In former days the additional word " humble " was added after " obedient " but Lord Curzon, when he became Foreign Secretary, considered this word inapplicable to the circumstances and it was thereafter abandoned. To a minister, the termination is identical except that the word " regard " is submitted for the word " respect." To a chargé d'affaires, both the respect and the regard are omitted and the line ends (somewhat curtly perhaps) with the word " truth."

In all urgent matters an envoy will communicate with his government by code telegram. These telegrams are also numbered. In recent years the telephone has also been much used in diplomatic communication.

On secondary matters, or matters of only technical importance, the envoy will report in the form of a memorandum (sometimes supplied by one of his staff) enclosed in a short covering despatch. Reports from consuls, or memoranda of incidental importance, are sent under cover of a " Printed Letter " drawn up in the third person.

In addition to these official despatches (which are entered in the Foreign Office registries and printed for circulation, if necessary, to the Cabinet and other missions abroad) there exists the practice of writing private letters by bag addressed either to the Secretary of State or to the Permanent Under-Secretary. Many controversies have arisen over the question whether such private correspondence is the property of the State or of the writers and recipients. Lord Salisbury, when he retired, took all his private letters with him down to Hatfield and considerable confusion was thereafter occasioned by gaps in correspondence. Sir Eyre Crowe, when Under-Secretary, had a prejudice against private letters and did his best to discourage the practice. Yet, in fact, there are many things which can be said in a private letter which could scarcely be said in the formality of an official despatch, and the practice, when not exaggerated or abused, is a useful one.

In his communications with the government to which he is accredited an ambassador will also adopt several different methods. There is the

Official Note which is signed and drafted in a conventional form. There is the Note Verbale which differs only from the Official Note by being unsigned. There are memoranda, and aide-mémoires. And there are verbal representations, which adopt every gradation of formality, from the official *démarche* to a casual conversation at some social function.

Those who have no experience of diplomacy, frequently wonder how an ambassador spends his time and what are the subjects on which he reports to his government. It will perhaps throw some light upon the functions of an envoy if I describe a typical twenty-four hours in an ambassador's life.

He will, if he is wise, begin his morning by dictating to his stenographer, in diary form, the events and conversations of the previous day. He will then read with care the local newspapers and consult with his Press attaché upon the significance of any given article. By that time his chancery will have decoded the telegrams which have come in overnight. These telegrams may contain instructions or ask for information and advice. He will draft his replies to these telegrams and, if necessary, fix an appointment with the Foreign Minister or Under-Secretary. The despatches and letters which have arrived by the morning's post will by then have been opened, entered in the registry, and minuted for suggested action by the staff. Matters affecting the military, naval, air, commercial or financial attachés will have been referred to them for their comments. The ambassador will read the more important of these despatches and letters and give instructions as to the action to be taken. By midday the interviews will begin. It may be that some foreign colleague comes to consult him, that some prominent journalist desires an interview, that a commercial magnate asks for assistance, that some consul has to come up to the capital to report or that some distressed fellow-citizen, either resident or travelling in the country, needs comfort and advice. A large proportion of the time of embassies and legations is absorbed by complaints of ill-usage on the part of their nationals.

In the afternoon the ambassador may see the Foreign Secretary and in that event he will need, immediately on his return, to write a report to his government while his memory is still fresh. More telegrams will have come in and more despatches have to be either read or written. An embassy has no regular hours and no week-ends. At moments of calm, there may be many hours for relaxation. In times of crisis every member of the staff is glad to work both day and night.

What, then, are the subjects which form the topic of all these reports, negotiations and despatches? Let us take as an example the envoy of a small power in London. There will be certain matters of direct interest to his country on which he will negotiate with the British Government. His government may desire a loan, or a reduction of the tariff on their exports, or British support at Geneva, or a word of warning to be given to one of their neighbours. All this will require a considerable amount of correspondence and many interviews. Yet in addition to this he is expected to keep his government informed of the main trends of British policy. He would be expected, for instance, to inform them of the parliamentary position of the government in power; of the strength of the opposition; of the attitude of the Trades Union Congress; of the relations between the Prime Minister and his colleagues; of the progress of the British armament programme; of the state of public opinion in regard to other Powers; of the condition of employment, health services and finances; of the incidence of taxation; of the cost of living; and, in fact, of any development or event which would enlighten his government on conditions and personalities in Great Britain, so as to enable them to base their policy upon a sure knowledge of existing facts and of probable future tendencies.

The social activities of an envoy are also of importance. He is expected to maintain a style commensurate with the dignity of the country he represents. He is expected to entertain frequently, to give large official dinner-parties and balls, and to invite officials, colleagues and men of business to constant informal meals. He is required to cultivate the intimacy of persons of eminence or influence in the country in which he resides; to display a lively interest in local industries, art, sport and letters; to visit the provinces and acquaint himself with industrial and agricultural conditions; and to keep in friendly contact with those of his countrymen who share his exile.

All this takes time.

V

Such then is the general life and procedure of the diplomatist. For the more detailed points of precedence or etiquette the reader is referred to Sir Ernest Satow's *Guide to Diplomatic Practice*. It remains, in concluding this chapter, to say a few words about the usual procedure at conferences and congresses.

The invitations to a conference are generally issued by the government of the country in which the conference is to be held. This rule is not always observed. The invitations to the Algeciras Conference were issued in the name of the Sultan of Morocco, although the Conference was held in Spain.

The delegates or plenipotentiaries nominated

by the several parties to the conference vary in status according to the importance of the subjects to be discussed. At the great conferences of history the Powers have usually been represented by their prime ministers or foreign secretaries. At minor conferences some diplomatist is generally chosen as delegate. For technical conferences it is usual to select specialists.

It is customary, although not obligatory, to elect as chairman of the conference the senior delegate of the country in which the conference is held. When the conference is held in a country which is not itself participating in the conference some difficulty is liable, under this heading, to arise. Thus the Lausanne Conference of 1922–23 was opened by the President of the Swiss Federation, who thereafter withdrew. A controversy then arose as to whether the British, French or Italian senior delegates should take the chair. A compromise was arranged under which each of the three should preside in turn. Lord Curzon evaded this compromise by insisting that it only applied to plenary sessions and not to sessions when the conference met as a committee. He then secured that it always *should* meet in committee, and as he was himself chairman of the main political committee he retained the chair at all but two meetings.

The Secretary General of a conference is usually

selected from among the officials of the country where the conference is held. When the conference takes place in a neutral country, the Secretary General is apt to be a member of the French delegation. He has under him a composite staff composed of the secretaries of the other delegations. The function of this body is to arrange the work of the conference, prepare the agenda, and above all to draft and circulate its minutes.

At important conferences, at which a large number of countries are represented, it is usual to restrict the plenary sessions to a few formal occasions. The subjects to be discussed are generally divided up into categories, and committees are appointed from among the several delegations to examine these subjects and to report to the main conference. The recommendations of these committees are usually put into proper form by a " Drafting Committee " consisting of expert jurists.

At the Paris Peace Conference an unusual and somewhat drastic method was employed. The Principal Allied and Associated Powers arrogated to themselves the whole conduct of the Conference, and formed themselves into a Council of Ten on which sat the first and second delegates of the five Great Powers. At a later date even this body was not found to be sufficiently exclusive and the direction of the Conference passed to the Council of Four, consisting of M. Clemenceau, President

Wilson, Mr. Lloyd George and Signor Orlando. The smaller Powers were only invited to attend the plenary sessions, which, in consequence, were few and very far between.

A difficult problem which arises at all conferences is the problem of publicity. The usual practice is for the conference to agree before the end of a meeting upon the terms of a communiqué to be issued to the Press. It invariably happens, however, that each delegation has its own pet correspondents to whom additional, and frequently quite inaccurate, information is divulged. Much bitterness and anxiety is caused by this inconvenience.

When agreement has been reached at a conference the results are embodied in a Treaty, Final Act, Convention or Protocol, and the signatures and seals of the several delegates are attached. The treaty is then handed over for safe custody to the Foreign Office of the country in which it has been signed. It is there also that the ratifications, if forthcoming, are eventually deposited.

CHAPTER IX

THE FOREIGN SERVICE

The British system—Origins of an organized diplomatic service—The reforms introduced from Pitt to Grey—The nomination system—The income qualification—Steps which a candidate should take to gain admission—The referees—The Selection Board—The examination—Ranks and salaries in the present Foreign Service—Differences between British and foreign practice—The German, French and American systems—The Consular Service—The problem of fusing all branches into one single service—Arguments in favour of such fusion

In previous chapters I have shown how, with increasing contact and communication between States, it was found useful to base international relations upon some recognized system of procedure and to entrust the execution of that procedure to a permanent staff of professional negotiators. That staff is to-day described as " the diplomatic service " or " the foreign service." In my present chapter I propose to examine how the British diplomatic service became an organized profession; what are the regulations which to-day govern its recruitment and internal organization and how the British system compares with that adopted in the United States, France and Germany.

No recognized diplomatic service existed in Great Britain until after the Congress of Vienna in 1815. "When I entered the service," wrote Lord Stratford de Redcliffe, "there was, so to speak, no such thing at all." In the eighteenth century there were only two Departments of State, which were called the Northern and the Southern Departments. These Departments dealt, upon no very stable system, both with external and internal affairs. When Pitt was Prime Minister he had two Under-Secretaries and nine clerks attached to his office, but their functions were as various as those which are now exercised by the Prime Minister's secretariat. In 1782 the Northern Department became the "Foreign Department," and in 1790, when this Department was transferred to Downing Street, the rudiments of a Foreign Office were created. A permanent Under-Secretary was appointed with a salary of £1,500 a year. He was assisted by a chief clerk, two senior clerks, nine junior clerks, a Latin secretary, and a "Decipherer of Letters." In 1822 this staff was increased and the first steps were taken to create a regular service of officials who would be attached to missions abroad.

Until that time it had been customary for an ambassador to select his own staff from such eligible young gentlemen as were personally recommended to him, much as a viceroy selects his aides-de-camp to-day. These young men were not paid by the State, although in exceptional cases they were accorded some expense allowance out of the ambassador's personal salary. They were housed and fed in the embassy and formed part of what was technically known as "the Ambassador's family."

This system of recruitment lingered on throughout the nineteenth century. In mid-Victorian times it was quite usual to find a secretary of embassy working upon a purely voluntary basis even after sixteen years of service. And so late as 1918 a young man who entered the Diplomatic Service was obliged to guarantee that for the first two years he would be possessed of a private income of not less than £400 a year. One of the most important recommendations of the Macdonnell Committee of 1914 was the abolition of this income qualification, and when in 1920 the whole scales of salary were adjusted so as to enable the junior members of the Diplomatic Service to support themselves without private means a great step was taken towards the democratization of the foreign service.

Originally the appointment, or nomination, of an attaché in the British diplomatic service rested entirely in the hands of the Secretary of State. The only qualifications demanded were the possession of a private income of not less than £400 and two months' probation in the Foreign Office.

In 1856 Lord Clarendon introduced an entrance examination with a high qualifying standard in French and handwriting. Under Lord Granville this qualifying examination was altered to a competitive examination. In 1871 a Select Committee recommended that candidates for the diplomatic service need only have an examination in handwriting provided they had taken their degree at Oxford or Cambridge. This recommendation was not adopted. In 1905 Lord Lansdowne changed the whole system of entry by decreeing that candidates for the Foreign Office or the Diplomatic Service should pass the usual Civil Service examination plus a high qualifying standard in French and German. A further reform was instituted by Sir Edward Grey in 1907 when he removed the selection of candidates for nomination from the hands of the Private Secretary and entrusted it to a "Selection Board" upon which outside bodies were represented. Until 1918 the Foreign Office and the Diplomatic Service had been regarded as separate organizations and a candidate could choose which of the two branches he desired to compete for. In July of that year Lord Cecil informed the House of Commons that in future these two branches would be fused into a single organization to be known as "The Foreign Service," and that the property qualification was henceforward to be abolished.

Such are the main changes which have been introduced into the British foreign service since the days of Pitt. It remains to examine what were the ideas behind these changes.

II

It will have been seen from the above that, until 1918, a young man could not become a member of the British foreign service until he had satisfied three main conditions, namely (1) guaranteed a personal income of £400 a year; (2) received a nomination entitling him to enter the examination; (3) passed the examination. Condition No. 1 has now been abolished; the nomination and the examination (although much altered) still remain.

Let us first discuss nomination. Under the old system, as it existed in Lord Clarendon's day, the examination was less important than the nomination. It has been said that the system led to nepotism and it would in fact be impossible to maintain it to-day. Yet it had its merits. In the first place the Secretary of State, before granting a nomination, took great pains to ascertain whether the young man in question was suited to a diplomatic career and likely to do credit to his country in that capacity. In the second place, having obtained his nomination and passed his qualifying test, he was only admitted as an attaché on probation. Whereas the nomination may have led to favouritism, and whereas the examination was largely a formality, the probation period was most exacting. It was possible for the head of a mission, by constant observation of an attaché, to report whether, at the end of his probation period, he should or should not be admitted as a salaried member of the profession. The percentage of rejections was a high one and it was this system of gradual "weeding-out" which provided Great Britain with her excellent ambassadors of 1880 to 1910.

The competitive system introduced by Lord Granville was not, in practice, an improvement on the former method. The old system of nomination remained in force, but the examination, instead of being a formality, became a very practical reality. Even as an examination, it was ill-conceived. An exacting standard was demanded in French, German, Italian, Spanish and geography. It thus became essential for any young man who hoped to prevail over other competitors (some of whom might be of mixed parentage and therefore bilingual) to spend some four years on the continent after leaving school. In the intervals of living in foreign families or pensions the candidates would cram geography at the institution of Mr. Scoones. The products of this system were not at all the products that the State required. It was found that these young men might be extremely proficient in languages, but that they knew little else. Nor was this all. It had been easy enough to weed out the probationers under the old system since their nomination as attachés had been merely an act of favour: it was far more difficult to reject a young man at the end of his probationary period if he had spent years of his youth in studying for a difficult competitive examination.

It was for this reason that in 1905 Lord Lansdowne insisted upon a candidate passing the ordinary Civil Service examination plus a qualifying examination in French and German. By reducing the amount of languages which must be taken and by insisting upon the ordinary Civil Service standard he drove his young candidates away from the Florence family or the Malaga pension and towards the more constructive discipline of the British universities. This was certainly an improvement.

The problem of nomination still remains. A candidate who wishes to enter the Foreign Service is still obliged to appear before a Selection Board before he can even enter the examination. This Board does not consist exclusively of members of the Foreign Service, but contains members of Parliament from all parties, a representative of the Civil Service Commission and a representative of the universities. The Board are not guided in their selection by social qualifications or charm; their sole aim is to nominate those young men who seem to possess the type of personality likely to be effective in modern diplomatic intercourse. Yet the fact remains that many candidates who might wish to present themselves for nomination are deterred by the legend that they will be judged only upon their social glamour or antecedents. It will be many years before that legend is killed.

III

What, therefore, are the practical steps which a young man should take if he desires to enter the British Foreign Service?

In the first place he should realize that the competition for entry is severe and that he has small chance of succeeding in the examination unless he has reached the standard of a good honours degree. The cramming establishments of England and the dancing-halls of the continent are littered with indolent young men who state that they are "studying for the diplomatic service." The parents of these young men should realize that they have little chance of gaining admission when they come up against competitors who may have gained honours at Oxford or Cambridge. They are merely wasting their time.

Supposing, however, that a youth of intelligence and industry is determined to compete for a post in the Foreign Service, his first action should be to write to the Secretary, Civil Service Commission,

Burlington Gardens, W.1, and ask to be furnished with the regulations governing application, nomination and examination. He will then receive a batch of perfectly legible instructions telling him exactly what he ought to do. He will probably find that his parents (who are unaware that the whole system has been changed) are convinced that the moment he leaves school he must plunge into the study of foreign languages. This is a dangerous illusion. The standard required in French and German to-day should be easily acquired by any gifted young man of ordinary application, provided that he spends his long vacations, and some six months after taking his degree, in France and Germany. What is essential is that his proficiency in the other subjects which he may select as his quota for the examination must be up to the standard of university honours. It will be difficult for him to attain that standard without attending the university. And, in fact, the boulevard or Italianate type of young Englishman is not the type which either the Foreign Office or the examiners desire to obtain.

Among the many papers which the applicant will receive from the Civil Service Commission will be an "Application Form." This form must be completed and sent to the Secretary of the Civil Service Commission not later than the first of March in the year in which the applicant wishes to appear before the Selection Board. By completing this form the aspirant asks to be admitted before the Selection Board at its next meeting on the first Tuesday in May following. He is required to give the obvious particulars regarding his age, nationality, education and so on. He is also expected to provide the names of two "referees" who shall be "responsible persons," but not relations or connected with the applicant's school or university.

This matter of referees occasionally causes some heart-burnings to the applicant and his parents. The old legend that the Board of Selection will be impressed if the two referees are of ducal rank has caused much distress to parents, the Board and the two dukes involved. The best type of referee is the man or woman whose name is likely to be known to the Board as that of a person of public experience and sound judgment. It is preferable for the applicant to have a solid if undistinguished referee who can state honestly that he has known the applicant for many years, than a decorative referee who merely says, "This young man is the son of one of my warmest supporters in my constituency." Referees with news-value are no good at all.

Having sent in his form of application, the aspirant will be informed that he will be interviewed by the Board at such and such a time on the first Tuesday in the following May. He will arrive punctually at Burlington Gardens with beads of perspiration on his brow. He should keep certain simple rules in mind. He should realize that the Board is composed of humane and experienced people who are perfectly well aware that he is passing through a grave ordeal and that he is not at his best. He should be very careful to avoid affectation, untruthfulness, ostentation or the more pungent brands of hair-wash. He will be unable to avoid self-consciousness, and a certain ingenuous bashfulness will not be out of place. He will not be asked difficult questions, but easy questions. He should reply to these questions as simply as possible, avoiding all epigram or paradox. He must remember above all that the whole purpose of the interview is to discover whether he be a young man of probity, character and common sense. If he bears these rules in mind, he may well receive his " nomination " or, as the phrase now goes, be " admitted to a competitive examination for appointment to the Foreign Office and Diplomatic Service."

The first problem that will then arise is the problem of age. A young man may appear before the Board of Selection any May after his nineteenth birthday. He cannot, however, take his examination unless he be over twenty-one or under twenty-five. It is advisable to appear before the Selection Board at a fairly early date, since, in the event of rejection, no time should be lost in deciding upon some other profession. A candidate who is not a British subject by birth, or who is married, or who has an extremely delicate constitution, had better not apply.

The examination generally takes place in July of each year and a candidate would be well advised to present himself the first July after his twenty-first birthday. If he fails, then he has three further chances before he is disqualified by having passed the age limit of twenty-five. The papers sent him by the Civil Service Commission will contain a syllabus of the examination with a statement of what marks are given for each subject. Certain subjects are obligatory. Every candidate must take French and German, a period of Modern History and Elementary Economics. He must also be examined in English and will have to write an essay upon some general subject. A very important feature of the examination is the Oral Examination, for which as many as 400 marks are given. This examination is in fact what the Americans call a "personality test."

Apart from these obligatory subjects, the candidate has a very wide range. He should realize from the outset that the examination as a whole has been devised to fit in with the university curriculum. Thus he will obviously take for his examination for the Diplomatic Service the same subjects as he took for his university degree, whether it be " Greats," Modern Greats, History, Classics, Mathematics or Modern Languages. The implication is that a university training is almost obligatory as a condition of entry. That would be to exaggerate the position. A very gifted and assiduous young man might possibly succeed in the examination without having set foot in any university in England, Scotland or Wales. Yet he would find himself competing with other candidates who had all the advantages of university tuition, and his battle would be a hard one.

When a candidate has successfully competed in the examination he is obliged to undergo a medical examination before final admission. This test should not prove insuperable for any youth of averagely sound constitution. Once he obtains his certificate of qualification, he can regard himself as a member of the foreign service. He will be informed by the Private Secretary of the Foreign Office where and when he should attend.

The old rank of attaché, under which a member of the foreign service worked for two years without pay, has now been abolished. A candidate who has been successful in the examination now enters directly as a Third Secretary with the salary attached to that grade. If working at home he will receive £275 a year, rising to £625. If he is serving abroad he will receive £300 from the first moment plus foreign allowance, which varies according to the expense of the post to which he has been appointed. These allowances are graded from £150 to £450 for a bachelor and from £300 to £650 for a married man. He will also receive a grant for local rent and a contribution to the expense of purchasing uniform.

After five years the Third Secretary is promoted a Second Secretary, but his pay and allowances are not increased. From that grade he passes, at specified, and at times at weary intervals, through the ranks of First Secretary, Counsellor, Minister or Under-Secretary until he becomes an Ambassador. On his retirement he will receive a pension proportionate to the rank he has attained.

IV

The methods of recruitment, entrance and appointment are not identical in every country.

In Germany, the Diplomatic and Consular Services are regarded as one. Candidates have to have the same qualifications for entry and they pass the same examination. A man thus spends a certain proportion of his career in a diplomatic mission and a certain portion as a member of a consulate or consulate-general. A candidate wishing to enter the German foreign service has to pass through several stages of probation. He must first pass a difficult examination in French and English.

He is then taken on for a year in the Foreign Office on probation. At the end of that year he has a second examination. If successful in that examination he is sent, again on probation, to a mission or a consulate abroad. He is then recalled to Berlin and, after three months' intense study, examined in international law, economics and history. Only then does he receive the title of "Attaché."

In France the system, which dates from 1875, is even more complicated. There are two types of examination, known respectively as "Le Grand Concours" and "Le Petit Concours." Those who are successful in the more difficult of these two examinations, either enter the Diplomatic Service as attachés, or become "Consuls Suppléants." Those who only take the easier of the two examinations become "Attachés de Consulat." The difference between the two types of consul is that whereas the first type become at once "Consuls of the third class," the second type have to pass through an intermediary stage of being Vice-Consuls.

The French system differs from the British system in that the gulf between the diplomatic and the consular services is less wide. The only difference is that promotion is more rapid for those who have taken the "Grand Concours" than for those who have only passed the "Petit Concours." Yet it is still possible for gifted men who have entered as "Attaché de Consulat" to reach to the very top, and M. Alphand, at present French Ambassador in Berne, started his career by passing the "Petit Concours."

The "Grand Concours" is a terrible ordeal. It lasts for some two months, and is conducted upon the "weeding-out" system. Thus the first examination is in the English and German languages, and counts for one quarter of the total marks. A candidate at this stage is examined by a committee of university professors presided over by a Counsellor of Embassy or a Consul-General.

If a candidate passes this first stage, he then enters the second stage which is called "le stage professionel." He has to appear before a committee of five members of the French foreign service, to write an essay and a précis and to pay visits of not less than ten minutes to each member of the committee. If he survives this ordeal he then has to take his final examination, which is conducted by university professors under the chairmanship of an ambassador. During this stage he is examined in history, geography and international law. This examination is both written and oral. The competition is generally severe, some fifty or sixty candidates competing for an average of five vacant posts.

The system now followed in the United States of

America is even more interesting. In the old days, before America became a World Power, it was customary to give diplomatic appointments as rewards for political services. To the more important posts men of ability and reputation were almost always appointed: yet it often occurred that some minor legation was awarded to a politician whose intelligence and conduct were not consonant with the dignity of the United States. Nor was this the only disadvantage of the "spoils system." The theory was that, since all diplomatic appointments were in the gift of the President, they should be surrendered when one President was succeeded by another. This meant that a change of administration brought with it a complete change in the diplomatic personnel. It thus came about that the American diplomatic service was staffed by a constant succession of temporary amateurs who often found themselves at a disadvantage when dealing with their professional colleagues. It was the blatant inefficiency and wastage of this system which led American public opinion to call for a reform in the direction of creating a professional foreign service staffed by permanent officials. This demand took effect in the "Reorganization Act of the American Foreign Service," which was first put into effect in May 1924.

Under this Act the diplomatic and consular services were fused into a single organization and the implication was that the service thus created would offer a good career to any ambitious young man. The entire service is to-day interchangeable as between the consular and the diplomatic branches, although in practice these interchanges occur more frequently in the lower grades of the service than in the higher.

The number of political appointments has meanwhile been reduced. Of the seventeen American embassies which exist to-day, nine are manned by career men who have been promoted through the ranks of the profession, one is now (September 1938) vacant, and seven are filled by political appointees. Of the thirty-nine separate American legations, two are vacant and of the remaining thirty-seven one half are manned by career men and one half by political appointees.

Recruitment for the American foreign service is a simple matter. Any young man is entitled to apply, but his application does not necessarily mean that he will be allowed to take the examination. The State Department examine the young man's credentials and his educational record and if these are unsatisfactory permission to stand for the examination is withheld. The examination is to-day very severe, and entails, as in Great Britain, a high standard of university education.

V

In Great Britain young men who do not feel that they are likely to compete successfully in the examination for the Diplomatic Service and the Foreign Office, and who yet desire to join some branch of the foreign service, may seek to enter either the Consular Service or the Assistant Officer grade in the Department of Overseas Trade.

The procedure which, in the event of that desire, they should follow is similar to that outlined above for entry into the foreign service. They should apply to the Secretary of the Civil Service Commission in Burlington Gardens and study the documents which he will send them. They also will have to pass through three stages, namely approval by a Board of Selection, a competitive examination and a medical examination. Candidates for the Consular Service will find that the competitive examination is less exacting than that laid down for diplomatic candidates, whereas the medical examination is more severe. Nor are the conditions of employment, salaries or allowances identical as between the two services.

The duties of a consular officer are not the same as those expected of a diplomatist. His main functions are commercial and notarial. He is expected to report upon commercial developments at his post and to furnish assistance and information to trade interests. A large part of his time will be taken up with assisting British shipping and seamen under the Merchant Shipping Acts and the Insurance Acts. He will also be required to register births, deaths and marriages and to deal with the awkward, and indeed painful, problem of the repatriation of distressed British subjects.

In the days of the capitulations, consuls also had judicial functions to perform. These are gradually dropping out of practice. Yet the glamour which, in eastern countries, hangs round the person of a consul has not as yet departed and there are many occasions upon which a consular official of intelligence and energy can furnish to his chiefs with the most valuable political information.

The British consular service is among the finest in the world. Complaints used in the past to be made that our consular officials did not furnish to their nationals that energetic support which the German and American officials were expected to accord. This criticism has now diminished, largely owing to the active impulse given to the consular service by the Department of Overseas Trade working through the Commercial Counsellors in the several embassies and legations.

In the British foreign service the diplomatic and the consular branches are not interchangeable and in fact a gulf is fixed between them. This, in my opinion, is a serious mistake. From time to time proposals have been made, and schemes advocated, under which the whole foreign service should be one large organism subject to the same rules of recruitment, examination and promotion. As yet, none of these schemes has come to fruition. The main difficulties are those of finance and vested interests. The financial problem, including the adjustment of salaries, is very serious, but could doubtless be surmounted were the Treasury convinced that fusion was necessary. The problem of vested interests is also a real one, but has been much exaggerated. The argument is that it would be unfair upon a man who had devoted much of his time and capital to reaching the standard of the diplomatic examination if he were suddenly placed on the same level as a man who had not made similar efforts or sacrifices. There is much force in this argument but it, also, is not insurmountable.

Under the present British system it is exceptional for a consul to reach diplomatic rank. Men of exceptional ability have, it is true, been appointed ambassadors from the ranks of the consular service. Such appointments are few, invidious, and far between. I am convinced none the less that the service as a whole would benefit were the two branches to be completely fused with each other. And for the following reasons.

The main weakness of the British Diplomatic Service, as of the Foreign Office, is the accumulation in the higher ranks of men who, although they have made no serious blunders and have displayed adequate judgment and energy, are not really fitted for the responsibilities of their posts. It is difficult to relieve such congestion without imposing hardship upon quite worthy people. On the other hand, the feeling that a solid wedge of worthies blocks promotion is apt to tempt the more ambitious man to leave the service while he is still young. This tendency is often exaggerated by outside observers who contend that the more ambitious men always leave. That is not true. But the fact remains that the more sedentary members of the profession acquire the conviction that they will eventually get their legation if only they avoid making mistakes; and that the more active members are sometimes discouraged by the vision of this large waiting-list among their official superiors.

The consular service on the other hand suffers from lack of opportunity and outlet for ambition. Things have been much improved during the last twenty years and the theory that the consular officials were necessarily the social and intellectual inferiors of the diplomatic officials has, I am glad to believe, largely died out. Yet faults remain. These faults would, in my judgment, be largely abolished if the two services were completely fused.

On the one hand you would obtain by this fusion a greater number of posts wherewith to satisfy your worthy incompetents and at the same time a larger number of posts whereby to encourage initiative and ambition in the young. Instead of feeling obliged to reward an elderly and indolent counsellor with the post of minister, it would be possible to award him the not undignified shelf of some consulate-general. Instead of stifling the initiative and ambition of a young vice-consul by blocking his rise to any but a consular post, you could hold out to him the prospect of becoming ambassador at some great capital. Even in the junior ranks of the service interchangeability would promote greater prowess. Had I myself spent two years as a Vice-Consul at Adana, I should have learnt much more about Turkey than I did as Third Secretary to the Embassy at Constantinople. Had the Vice-Consul at Adana spent one year, on completely equal terms with the embassy staff, at Constantinople, he would have acquired greater political and social acumen. No arguments will convince me that the fusion of the two services would not be of great advantage to both.

Yet there is one condition which I should make. The advantage of the old diplomatic service was that, being a small group of men, it was possible for those in whose hands lay the appointments to have a shrewd idea of the personal value of each member. If the service were enlarged by fusion, this personal method of appraisal would become less certain and more fortuitous. A filter would thus have to be devised. For this purpose I should suggest some institution analogous to the Staff College. Under such a system young men of the joint or amalgamated foreign service would be obliged, after say eight years of service, to decide whether or no they would enter for the Staff College. It would generally be understood that only those who passed through the Staff College course would be eligible for the higher appointments. The course would in itself be devised to increase the economic and political knowledge of those who underwent it. And you would thereby get an élite drawn from the whole service from which, without invidious personal discriminations, the higher posts could be filled.

Yet, such is human frailty, it may be many years before this essential reform has been achieved.

CHAPTER X

DIPLOMATIC LANGUAGE

The expression " diplomatic language " as implying cautious under-statement—Advantages and disadvantages of " diplomatic language "—Latin as the original common language of diplomacy—Gradually superseded by French—Decline after the war in the use of the French language—Its suitability as a diplomatic medium—Diplomatic phrases which are becoming obsolete—Glossary of some current diplomatic expressions

THE expression " diplomatic language " is used to denote three different things. In its first sense it signifies the actual language (whether it be Latin, French, or English) which is employed by diplomatists in their converse or correspondence with each other. In its second sense it means those technical phrases which, in the course of centuries, have become part of ordinary diplomatic vocabulary. And in its third, and most common, sense it is used to describe that guarded under-statement which enables diplomatists and ministers to say sharp things to each other without becoming provocative or impolite.

I propose in this chapter to begin by discussing the last of these three meanings, then to examine shortly the actual language employed by diplomatists, and at the end to provide a glossary of the more current technical terms used in diplomatic intercourse.

" Diplomacy," if I may repeat Sir Ernest Satow's definition, " is the application of intelligence and tact to the conduct of official relations between the governments of independent states." The need of intelligence is self-evident, but the equally vital need of tact is often disregarded. It is this latter need which has led diplomatists to adopt a paper currency of conventionalized phrases in place of the hard coins of ordinary human converse. These phrases, affable though they may appear, possess a known currency value.

Thus, if a statesman or a diplomatist informs another government that his own government " cannot remain indifferent to " some international controversy, he is clearly understood to imply that the controversy is one in which his government will certainly intervene. If in his communication or speech he uses some such phrases as " His Majesty's Government view with concern " or " view with grave concern," then it is evident to all that the matter is one in which the British Government intend to adopt a strong line. By cautious gradations such as these a statesman is enabled, without using threatening language, to convey a serious warning to a foreign government. If these warnings pass unheeded he can raise his voice while still remaining courteous and conciliatory. If he says, " In such an event His Majesty's Government would feel bound carefully to reconsider their position," he is implying that friendship is about to turn into hostility. If he says " His Majesty's Government feel obliged to formulate express reservations regarding . . ." he is, in fact, saying " His Majesty's Government will not allow . . ." The expression " in that event, my Government will be obliged to consider their own interests," or " to claim a free hand," indicates that a rupture of relations is being considered. If he warns a foreign government that certain action on their part will be regarded " as an unfriendly act," that government interpret his words as implying a threat of war. If he says that " he must decline to be responsible for the consequences," it means that he is about to provoke an incident which will lead to war. And if he demands, even in terms of exquisite politeness, a reply before " six o'clock on the evening of the 25th," then his communication is rightly regarded as an ultimatum.

The advantage of this conventional form of communication is that it maintains an atmosphere of calm, while enabling statesmen to convey serious warnings to each other which will not be misunderstood. The disadvantage is that the public and sometimes even the statesmen themselves, are not acquainted with the actual value, in diplomatic currency, of the expressions used. On the one hand an ignorant or incautious use of one of these phrases may give to a given situation a gravity which it does not possess. On the other hand, when a really serious crisis arises, the public is apt to assume from the mildness of the language used that the crisis cannot be as grave as " the alarmists " had given them to suppose.

In extreme cases, moreover, the habit of diplomatic ambiguity, or of diplomatic understatement, leads to actual misunderstanding. I remember before the war reading a despatch from some Consul-General in which he informed the Foreign Office that one of the Vice-Consuls under his charge " does not, I much regret to report, take that care of his health which his medical advisers would recommend." The poor man was, in fact, in the last stages of *delirium tremens*.

Such exaggeration of the practice is not common, and in all important international controversies these paper-currency phrases are most carefully scrutinized before they are used. It may be said that the advantages of phrasing communications between governments, or important pronouncements on foreign affairs, in " diplomatic language " far outweigh any disadvantages which the system may possess.

II

Until the eighteenth century the common language, or *lingua franca* of diplomacy was Latin. Not only did diplomatists write to each other in Latin but they even conversed in that medium. Such treaties as those of Westphalia (1648), the Anglo-Danish Treaty of 1670, and the Anglo-Dutch Treaty of 1674 were all drafted and signed in Latin and this was in fact the general practice. During the course of the eighteenth century the French made repeated efforts to secure the adoption of their own language as the language of diplomacy. These efforts were stubbornly resisted by the other Powers. Thus, although the Treaty of Aix-la-Chapelle of 1748 was signed in French, a special article was inserted to the effect that this was not to create a precedent. A similar reservation was, at the insistence of the other signatory Powers, inserted into the Treaty of Paris of 1763, the Treaty of Versailles of 1783, and even in the Final Act of the Congress of Vienna.

In spite of these reservations, the French language had, by the middle of the eighteenth century, firmly established itself as, in all but name, the official language of diplomacy. At the Congress of Vienna in 1815 and the Congress of Paris in 1856 the proceedings were conducted in French throughout. It was in fact not until the Paris Conference of 1918–19 that English was given equality of rights with French. " The Present Treaty "—thus runs the ratification clause of the Treaty of Versailles—" of which the French and English texts are both authentic. . . ." It was that clause which finally disposed of the claim of French to be the official language of negotiation.

This was perhaps inevitable. It was evident that the supremacy of the French language gave to French diplomatists an advantage over their colleagues. In the days of the old diplomacy, when the diplomatists of all countries were obliged to be almost bilingual, this advantage was not so preponderant. But with the advent of democratic diplomacy, and the frequent handling of negotiations by the elected representatives of the people, it became a practical impossibility to converse in French. Sir Edward Grey, for instance, could scarcely speak French, although he claimed to understand it. President Wilson and Mr. Lloyd George were no linguists, and the practice thus arose that the representative of each country could, if he desired, speak in his own language, his words being thereafter translated by an interpreter. This practice has not proved so inconvenient as many suppose. A trained interpreter can translate a statement or a speech with great lucidity and speed; Professor Mantoux, who interpreted during the Paris Conference, brought to his task a touch of genius. The delay entailed is not inconvenient to a negotiator who, having gathered the gist of the previous remarks, is able, during the period of translation, to ruminate on his own reply.

It was not only in conferences and congresses that French held its supremacy. Ordinary diplomatic intercourse was, until the Treaty of Versailles, conducted almost exclusively in that language. The Far East, where English was the common tongue, was an exception to this rule. In Europe the whole process of notes, memoranda, and official or social conversation, was conducted in the French language. In the Russian diplomatic service of Tsarist days many of the Russian Ambassadors used French in their despatches to their own government. And to this day, throughout Europe, it is customary to accept French as the current medium of diplomatic intercourse.

It is in some ways to be regretted that the old practice is disappearing. It is of obvious convenience that there should exist some common language in which Lithuanians can converse with Portuguese, or Greeks with Danes. The absence of such a generally accepted medium of communication leads to difficulties. The Embassy of a Great Power in London recently issued invitations for an official reception in its own nordic tongue. The representative of a Middle Eastern potentate replied to this invitation in Arabic. It was only with difficulty that the Ambassador could discover whether his guest had accepted or refused.

Nor can it be questioned that the French language possesses qualities which entitle it to claim precedence over others for all purposes of diplomatic intercourse. It is impossible to use French correctly without being obliged to place one's ideas in the proper order, to develop them in a logical sequence, and to use words of almost geometrical accuracy. If precision is one of the major virtues of diplomacy, it may be regretted that we are discarding as our medium of negotiation one of the most precise languages ever invented by the mind of man.

III

I now pass to a definition of some of the more technical phrases employed in current diplomatic usage. One may observe incidentally that many of the expressions which were of common usage in the nineteenth century are now obsolete. No Secretary of State would to-day refer to his colleagues in the Cabinet as " His Majesty's Servants." The phrase " The European System " is to-day devoid of meaning, while even the " Concert of Europe " scarcely survived the European War. Diplomatists no longer describe the German or the Soviet Governments as " The Northern Courts." The Russian Ambassador is no longer referred to by the Kremlin as " our Ambassador at the Court of St. James'." It would cause bewilderment if a minister were to refer, as Wellington referred, to a massacre as " the transactions complained of." And the confusion which occurs over the use of the title " Excellency " would have much distressed a diplomatist of the pre-war vintage.

A welcome change is the decline in the practice (so dear to the foreign correspondents of English newspapers) of calling the several Foreign Offices by pet names. We still, occasionally, speak of the French Foreign Office as " The Quai d'Orsay," and of its German counterpart as " The Wilhelmstrasse." Yet " The Haus am Ballplatz " is no more: and the expression " The Sublime Porte " (which even in its halcyon days was a mistranslation of the words " Bab Ali " or " Gate of Sublimity ") will shortly be recognizable only by students of diplomatic history.

I now pass to my glossary. My main authority for the definitions given is Sir Ernest Satow's classic work, *A Guide to Diplomatic Practice*, a revised edition of which was published in 1932, after having been scrupulously brought up to date by Mr. H. Ritchie.

ACCESSION. It is a frequent practice to insert an " accession clause " into an international treaty under which Powers who were not represented at the negotiations and who did not sign the original treaty can " accede " to it later. A good instance is Article 22 of the International Opium Convention of January 23, 1912, which provides that " Powers who have not been represented at this Conference shall be admitted to sign the present Convention."

ACCORD. Matters of general international concern which are not of sufficient importance to justify a formal treaty or convention are frequently arranged by means of an " accord " or " agreement." The subjects dealt with by such agreements are copyright, public health, pharmacopœial formulas, and so on.

ACTE FINAL. It often occurs that at the conclusion of some conference or congress it is found convenient to draw up some formal summary or statement of its proceedings. Such statements enumerate the treaties signed as a result of the conference, and often contain certain expressions of opinion, or agreed comments, on the subjects discussed. Such a summary is sometimes called " Acte," " Protocol," or " Procès Verbal Final." But the expression " Acte Final " is more correct.

AD REFERENDUM. A negotiator often finds it convenient to accept some proposition on the part of those with whom he is negotiating without committing his own government. He therefore accepts it " ad referendum," meaning thereby " subject to the approval of my government."

AGRÉMENT OR AGRÉATION. When one government wishes to accredit an ambassador or a minister to another government, it is necessary that the individual selected should be approved by the government of the country to which he is being sent. It is customary, in order to avoid personal embarrassments, to sound a foreign government privately before making a formal application for an agrément. A famous instance of an agrément having been withheld was when the Emperor Nicholas of Russia refused to accept Sir Stratford Canning as British Ambassador in St. Petersburg.

ASYLUM. It is generally accepted practice that a political refugee who takes asylum in a foreign country should not be deported back to his own country from which he has escaped. A more difficult question arises when a political refugee takes asylum, not in a foreign country, but in a foreign embassy or legation in his own capital. In some Oriental countries, notably in Persia, this system is much abused and whole tribes of politicians and their families take refuge or "*bast*" in a Legation compound in order to escape the vengeance of their master. Prolonged negotiations are often necessary before such refugees can be induced to depart.

ATTACHÉ. There are three types of attaché. The first are naval, military, air or commercial attachés who are generally senior officers and who are attached to a mission for specialized services. The second are diplomatic attachés who represent the lowest grade of diplomatic secretaries. Of recent years this grade has in many countries been abolished and the name of attaché changed to Third Secretary. The third type is that of the Honorary Attaché, who is an unpaid volunteer, who is not a permanent member of the service, but who is generally a young man of private means and excellent connections who spends a space of time in an embassy or legation between finishing his university career and settling down to the serious business of life.

BAG, THE. An ambassador or minister communicates with his government either by cypher telegram, by telephone, or in the form of written reports and despatches. The latter are placed in mail bags which are carried by special couriers or "King's Messengers." Occasionally the Foreign Office bags are entrusted to the safe keeping of the captains of British vessels and the whole courier service has of late been much reduced. The King's Messengers or couriers are provided with special passports and their bags are inviolable. In the old days members of missions abroad were allowed to send and receive "by favour of the bag" not only their private correspondence but a large number of commodities. This privilege has now been much restricted in so far as the British diplomatic service is concerned. The day on which "the bag" arrives or leaves is always one of great activity in missions abroad. It is called "bag-day." The French use a similar expression—"la valise."

BELLIGERENT RIGHTS. This expression is one which concerns international law rather than diplomatic practice. Under international law a government which is engaged in war possesses certain recognized rights and duties. The most important of these rights is that which enables them to declare a blockade of the coasts and ports of their enemy. Insurgents and revolutionaries do not possess these rights until they are recognized as "belligerents." The general practice has been to grant belligerent rights to insurgents the moment it is clear that the situation has passed from the stage of a rebellion into the stage of a civil war. But there is no absolute rule governing such procedure.

BILATERAL. See under Treaties.

CAPITULATIONS. The Powers were able in the course of centuries to impose treaties on certain non-Christian countries, under which their own nationals residing in the country should enjoy special privileges and immunities. Among these privileges was exemption from taxation and from trial by native courts. These treaties were called " Capitulations " and the whole infinitely complicated system was called " The Capitulatory System." The Powers who enjoyed the benefits of such treaties were called the " Capitulatory Powers " as distinct from those smaller Powers who were outside the system. After the war, Turkey and Persia abolished the capitulations with the consent of the Powers.

CASUS BELLI. A casus belli is an act committed by one country against another country of such a nature as to justify war. Thus the invasion of Egypt by a foreign Power would be regarded by Great Britain as a casus belli.

CASUS FŒDERIS. A casus fœderis is different from the above. It means some action or event which brings into operation a particular treaty of alliance and justifies one party to that treaty in calling upon another party to come to his assistance. A German invasion of Czechoslovakia would have constituted a casus fœderis in that the Czech Government could then have called upon the French and Russian Governments to fulfil their treaty obligations.

CHANCELLERIES. A confusion is often made between

the word " Chancellery " and the word " Chancery." A chancellery was originally the secretariat of a chancellor. It is now employed only to designate those ministers and officials who control, or advise upon, foreign policy. The phrase " The Chancelleries of Europe " is in practice indistinguishable from the phrase " The Foreign Offices of the Powers." The word " Chancery " designates the actual office of a head of a diplomatic mission, namely his first, second and third secretaries, plus the attendant clerks. It is also used to designate the premises in which they exercise their functions. A " Chancery Servant " corresponds to the " Office Messenger " in a government department.

CHARGÉ D'AFFAIRES. When an ambassador or minister goes on leave he entrusts the conduct of his mission to the next senior officer of the staff, either the counsellor or the first secretary. This official becomes, for the time being, head of the mission, conducts negotiations with the foreign government, and reports to his own government. On occasions when it is desired to manifest displeasure with a foreign government the chargé d'affaires is maintained for a long period and no successor to the departed ambassador or minister is appointed. No agrément is required in the case of a chargé d'affaires.

COMPROMIS D'ARBITRAGE. When two countries agree to submit a dispute to arbitration it may be found convenient to draw up a compact defining the course of procedure to be followed. This compact is called a " Compromis d'Arbitrage," or more usually a " Compromis."

CONCORDAT. When the Pope signs a treaty with the head of a State it is called a " concordat." These treaties begin with the words " In the name of the Most Holy and Indivisible Trinity." One of the most striking of recent concordats is that between the Pope and the King of Italy for the settlement of the " Roman Question," which was signed at the Lateran on February 11, 1929.

CONFERENCE AND CONGRESS. There is no accepted difference between these two words. It is sometimes contended that a congress is a more important version of a conference, or that the word " congress " is used when territory is redistributed after a general war, or when practically all the Great Powers are represented. History does not show that such distinctions have been made in practice, for whereas there was the Congress of Vienna, the discussion held in Paris after the war of 1914–18 was styled a " conference." It might be argued with greater justification that the word " conference " is more applicable to meetings at which only the victors in a war, or the directly interested parties, are represented, and that when both the conquered countries and neutral countries are admitted the word " congress " is more correct. Even this distinction would be questioned by purists.

CONVENTION. A convention is a less important form of treaty, namely one which is concluded, not between heads of States, but between governments.

CORPS DIPLOMATIQUE. The diplomatic body in any capital is composed of the diplomatic staffs of the several missions, including the attachés. Consuls and student interpreters are not generally regarded as forming part of the body. The senior ambassador or minister becomes the " dean " or " doyen " of the diplomatic body, and represents them in any disputes affecting their corporate rights and interests.

COUNSELLOR. The senior secretary at an embassy (and in exceptional cases at a legation) has the title of " Counsellor " (" conseiller," " Botschaftsrat "). At important embassies, such as those in Paris and Washington, the Counsellor is given the rank of Minister. It is he who, in the absence of the head of a mission, acts as " Chargé d'Affaires."

CREDENTIALS. An ambassador or minister is, on being appointed to a post, provided with Credentials, or Letters of Credence, signed by his sovereign or the head of his State. Until he has formally " presented his letters " he is not officially recognized.

DÉMARCHE. The closest English equivalent for the expression " faire une démarche " is " make representations," but it should be remembered that the word in French covers all manner of representations from proposals to threats.

DÉTENTE. The word " détente " is not, as some people suppose, the opposite of " entente." It simply means " a relaxation of tension."

DIPLOMATIC ILLNESS. It is frequently convenient for a statesman or a negotiator to absent himself from some ceremony or meeting. In order not to cause undue offence, he pleads illness. In cases where this malady is a feigned pretext it is called " diplomatic."

DIPLOMATIC PRIVILEGE. Members of diplomatic missions are accorded certain privileges and immunities in the countries where they reside officially. These privileges are given, not merely to the head of the mission, but to his staff, their wives and families, and his servants. They include such immunities as inviolability of person and domicile, exemption from local taxation and from local criminal and civil jurisdiction. A member of the diplomatic body cannot be summoned, sued or forced to give witness in a court of law. He may be asked to "waive his diplomatic privilege," but he is not obliged to comply with such a request. In extreme cases (which, for diplomatists are a mild race, are fortunately rare) the government of the country in which a diplomatist has committed a criminal offence can demand his recall and can even arrest him once he has been divested of his official status. Diplomatic privilege is sometimes extended to persons (such as members of the League Secretariat) who are not technically diplomatists.

EN CLAIR. A telegram is sent either in secret code or in ordinary language. If the latter, it is called a telegram "en clair." Such messages are sent when it is intended that the local government should read the message without undue trouble.

ENTENTE. This expression arose from the phrase "entente cordiale" or "cordial understanding." It implies, as does the new word "axis," a similarity of views and interests between certain countries and an identity of policy upon certain issues. It thus stands half-way between an "alliance" and "good relations." During the war and subsequently the term was used concretely to describe those Powers who were united by this form of understanding, e.g. "Triple Entente," "Balkan Entente," etc.

Excellency. In Great Britain this foolish title is accorded only to Ambassadors, Viceroys and Governors-General. In foreign countries it is extended to Cabinet Ministers and to all those, of a certain age and standing, whom it is desired to please.

Exterritoriality. This word is loosely used to define the diplomatic privileges and immunities referred to above. See also under Capitulations.

Extradition. Under the Extradition Treaties in force between almost every country in the world a criminal who escapes to a foreign country is "extradited" to the country in which the crime was committed. Political offences do not come within the scope of extradition treaties and political fugitives, once they make good their escape, are granted "asylum."

"Extraordinary." In the old days there existed a distinction between "ordinary," or resident ambassadors, and "extraordinary" ambassadors despatched on special missions. This led to invidious distinctions, and all ambassadors are now "extraordinary."

"Fin De Non Recevoir." An expression which is used to describe the diplomatic practice of rejecting an official complaint without examining into its merits. When a diplomatist says that his representations were met by a "fin de non recevoir" he is saying much the same as "they absolutely refused to take up the case."

Full Powers. A negotiator, before he signs an international treaty, is provided with "full powers" signed and sealed by his sovereign. If he is only signing a convention his "full powers" are signed by the Secretary of State. In Great Britain a royal "full power" assures "all and singular to whom these Presents shall come" that "reposing especial Trust, and Confidence in the Wisdom, Loyalty, Diligence and Circumspection of Our Trusty and well-beloved Sir X. Y. . . . etc. etc. have named, made, constituted and appointed him Our undoubted Commissioner, Procurator and Plenipotentiary in respect of Great Britain and Northern Ireland."

General Act. A General Act is either a summary of the conclusions of a conference or detailed regulations deriving from certain principles embodied in a treaty.

Good Offices. In the event of a controversy or war arising between two countries it often happens that a third country uses its "good offices" for the purpose, either of easing the controversy or facilitating peace negotiations. Good offices differ from mediation in degree only. A government which places its "good offices" at the disposal of two conflicting parties is doing little more than acting as a channel of communication : mediation is a far more formal method, and implies that the mediator will actually conduct negotiations himself.

Guarantee, Treaties of. Certain treaties contain clauses under which the signatories guarantee their execution and maintenance. Thus under the Treaty of London of 1839 we guaranteed the integrity of Belgium and it was in execution of this pledge that we made war in 1914. A great difference exists between a "collective guarantee" and a "joint and several guarantee." In the former case (as in the case of our guarantee under the 1867 Treaty of Luxemburg integrity) a signatory is only obliged to take action if all the other signatories do the same. Conversely, a "joint and several" guarantee (as, it was contended, had been given to Belgium in 1839) obliges every signatory to take action even if the other signatories evade or violate their obligations.

LAISSER PASSER. Officials when travelling on business are accorded by the embassy of the country which they intend to visit a letter of recommendation to the customs authorities. This ensures that their luggage will not be examined at the frontier. British missions abroad are discouraged from granting laisser passers to any but actual officials when travelling on official business. Other countries are more generous in granting these facilities.

MÉMOIRE. Apart from the formal Notes (see later) addressed by the head of a mission to a foreign government, there are varying types of memoranda which differ from Notes in that they begin with no formal introduction and need not be signed. Several names are given to such documents—"pro-mémoria," "déduction" or "exposé de motifs." Another form is the "aide-mémoire," which is a short memorandum handed by an ambassador to a Foreign Secretary at the end of an interview in which a short written summary is given of the oral representations which he has been instructed to make.

MISE EN DEMEURE. When government "A" faces government "B" with a curt "take it or leave it" demand, or insists upon a definition of intentions, it is called a m.e.d.

MODUS VIVENDI. A name given to a temporary agreement which it is intended to replace later on by a more formal and precise convention.

NOTES. The ordinary diplomatic Note is a formal communication from the head of a mission to a government which may be written either in the first or the third person. Variations of the ordinary Note are: (*a*) *Collective Note.* This is a Note addressed to a government by the representatives of several States in regard to a matter on which they have been instructed to make "joint representations." A "Collective Note" is seldom signed by all participating ambassadors on the same sheet, but each ambassador sends in his own Note, the text being identical. On very solemn occasions these Notes are presented simultaneously by the ambassadors concerned. (*b*) *Identic Note.* An "Identic Note" is similar to a Collective Note but less overwhelmingly impressive. The text, as distinct from the substance, need not be identical and the Identic Note need not be presented simultaneously. (*c*) *Note Verbale.* This is a type of communication which is less formal than a signed Note and more formal than a memorandum. It is unsigned, but it is customary that it should contain at the end some conventional expression of courtesy. It is, in fact, merely the addition of this polite tag which differentiates it from the mémoire.

PERSONA GRATA. When an ambassador or other envoy becomes intolerably obnoxious to the government to which he is accredited, it is said that he has ceased to be a "persona grata." This amounts to a request for his recall. Thus Bulwer, who had ventured to give advice to the Spanish Government regarding their internal politics, was asked by Sotomayor "to anticipate as much as possible the leave of absence he was contemplating." Bulwer replied that he had no such "leave of absence" in his mind. He was then handed his passports and told to go. Palmerston thereupon broke off diplomatic relations with Spain and dismissed the Spanish Minister in London.

PLACEMENT. Although the old wrangles about precedence have diminished in intensity, diplomatists are still much exercised by the order in which they sit at a dinner-party. The science of seating diplomatic guests in such a manner as to avoid enraging them is called the science of "placement."

PRENDRE ACTE is a diplomatic way of saying "I shall take note of this and bring it up against you in the future."

PROCÈS VERBAL. The "minutes" of a conference. If signed by the participants, such minutes acquire binding force.

PROTOCOL. Originally a protocol was a mere record of agreement and as such far less formal than a treaty or convention. Yet many very important international compacts have taken this form, notably the agreement signed in 1920 at Geneva establishing the Permanent Court of International Justice.

PROTOCOLE. There is no exact English translation of the word "protocole." It combines our "correct form of procedure" and "ceremonial." Thus the Chef du Protocole abroad corresponds on one side to our Lord Chamberlain and on the other to the head of the Treaty Department of the Foreign

Office. The adjective "protocolaire" is used for a stickler for conventional forms.

RAISON D'ÉTAT. The diplomatic and political theory under which the interests of the State take precedence over all private morality.

RAPPORTEUR. When a committee or sub-committee has been appointed by a conference to consider some specific matter, they choose one of their number to be their spokesman with the main conference and to present their report. He is called a "rapporteur."

RECOGNITION, De FACTO. When an insurgent is sufficiently successful to establish his administration over an important area of a country he is usually recognized by foreign Powers as the "de facto" or actual, as distinct from the "de jure," or legitimate, ruler of that area. Similarly in war a State occupying and administering large areas of enemy country is regarded as the "de facto" authority in those areas.

SAFE-CONDUCT is permission for an individual to pass without let or hindrance through the territory of his country's enemies. Thus Count Bernstorff in 1917 was given a safe-conduct by the Allies to enable him to return to Germany from the United States.

SANCTIONS. Penalties inflicted for a breach of a law or of the covenant.

STATUS QUO. The expression "status quo" is used to denote the situation as it existed at a particular moment. In former diplomatic language, when referring to territories possessed by a sovereign at any given date the phrase was "*uti possidetis.*" "*Status quo ante bellum,*" or "*status quo ante*" merely means the situation as it was before the war.

TREATIES. Treaties are either "bilateral," or concluded between two countries only, or "militlateral," or concluded between several countries. Treaties of "mutual guarantee" are those international compacts which, as the Treaties of Locarno, aim at guaranteeing each signatory against attack from another.

ULTIMATUM. The word "ultimatum" is sometimes regarded as meaning "declaration of war." This is incorrect. It is often merely "the last word" before a negotiation is broken off. It generally takes the form of a written intimation that unless a satisfactory reply is received by a certain hour on a certain date certain consequences will follow. These consequences are not necessarily war. Thus Palmerston, in the unfortunate affair of Don Pacifico, presented an ultimatum to Greece in which he informed them that if they did not accept his terms within twenty-four hours he would seize Greek ships and blockade the coasts of Greece.

UNDER FLYING SEAL. It often happens that an ambassador in sending a report home to his government thinks that it would be useful if the information therein contained were communicated to a colleague in some other capital. He thus sends the despatch "under flying seal," which only means that the second ambassador reads it on its way through. Thus a despatch from the British Ambassador in St. Petersburg would, if marked "under flying seal to Berlin," be opened and read on its way through to the Foreign Office by the British Ambassador in the latter capital.

UNFRIENDLY ACT. When a State wishes to warn other States that certain actions on their part might lead to war, it is usual to state that such action would "be regarded as an unfriendly act."

UNILATERAL DECLARATION. Occasionally Powers seek to establish their rights or policy by a declaration of principle which is communicated to other Powers for their information and guidance. The Monroe Doctrine was in effect such a declaration. A more recent example was Lord Curzon's circular Note to the Powers, of March 15, 1922, in which he warned them that Great Britain "would not admit" the special relations existing between herself and Egypt to be questioned or discussed by any other Power and would regard any attempt at intervention in Egypt as "an unfriendly act."

VENUE. This expression is not employed by experienced diplomatists, but is much used by journalists. It signifies the place where a conference or meeting is held. It is considered by professional diplomatists rather vulgar to use this debased word.

VOEUX. It sometimes happens that a conference wishes to add to its treaty certain "recommendations" for future good conduct. These are called "wishes" or "voeux." Thus the Hague Peace Conference of 1899 emitted six "voeux." These have no binding force upon the signatories.

BIBLIOGRAPHY

The standard work on diplomatic practice is *Guide to Diplomatic Practice*, by Sir Ernest Satow. This admirable work has been revised and brought up to date in its third edition by Mr. H. Ritchie. Much valuable information will also be found in the Cambridge History of British Foreign Policy.

Other books recommended are :

The Diplomatist, by Jules Cambon.
Diplomacy and Peace, by Professor R. B. Mowat.
Enfances diplomatiques, by W. d'Ormesson.
Envoys Extraordinary, by Edmund d'Auvergne.
The Foreign Office, by Sir John Tilley.
Foundations of British Foreign Policy, by Temperley and Penson.
International Relations, by Professor R. B. Mowat.
The Spirit of British Policy, by Professor Kantorowicz.
Our Foreign Affairs, by Paul Scott Mowrer.
Traité de diplomatie, by Count Szilassy.
Vatican Diplomacy, by Count de Salis.
School of Ambassadors, by Jusserand.

INDEX

Printed by The Riverside Press, Edinburgh

4 Make up your own sentences using pictures to help you.

The time of day

Dîner
Dinner

C'est le soir.
It is evening.

Il est l'heure
se coucher.
It's time to go to bed.

5 Read and learn the words in the speech bubble at the bottom of the page and try them out with your friends.

6 Test yourself! Cover the words, look at the picture and say or spell the French word.

Written by Amanda Doyle

Illustrated by Ian Cunliffe

Educational Consultant: Jo Crocombe

A catalogue record for this book is available from the British Library

Published by Ladybird Books Ltd
80 Strand, London, WC2R 0RL
A Penguin Company

2 4 6 8 10 9 7 5 3 1

ISBN: 978-140930-224-7

Printed in China

HELPERS

French for School

Je me présente

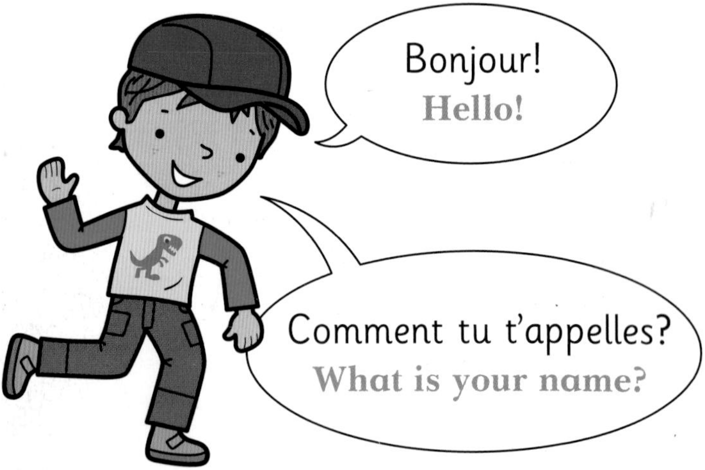

About me

Quel âge as-tu?
How old are you?

J'ai sept ans.
I am seven years old.
Au revoir!
Goodbye!

1 un

2 deux

3 trois

4 quatre

5 cinq

6 six

7 sept

8 huit

9 neuf

10 dix

Voici ma famille.
Here is my family.
Salut!
Hi!
ma soeur
My sister
mon père
My father
ma mère
My mother

ma grand-mère

My grandmother

mon grand-père

My grandfather

mon frère

My brother

L'heure de la journée

Il est l'heure
de se lever.
It's time to get up.

C'est le matin.
It is morning.

Petit déjeuner
Breakfast

Déjeuner
Lunch

C'est l'après-midi.
It is afternoon.

The time of day

Dîner

Dinner

C'est le soir.

It is evening.

Il est l'heure
se coucher.
It's time to go to bed.

Le temps

Quel temps fait-il?
What's the weather like?

Il fait beau.
It's fine.

Il pleut.
It's raining.

Il géle.
It's freezing.

Weather

Il neige.
It's snowing.

Il fait chaud.
It's hot.

Il fait froid.
It's cold.

Il y a du vent.
It's windy.

Il y a du soleil.
It's sunny.

Le pique-nique

Dans le sac, il y a...
In the bag there is/are...

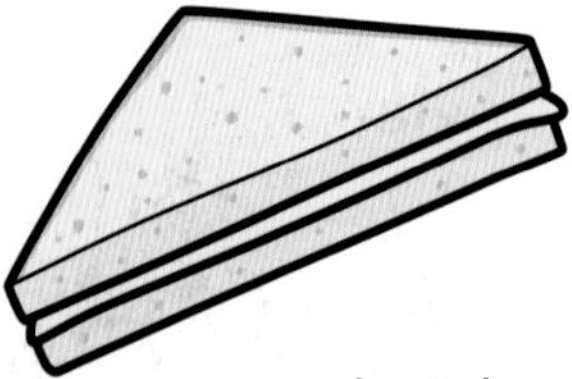

un sandwich
au fromage
a cheese sandwich

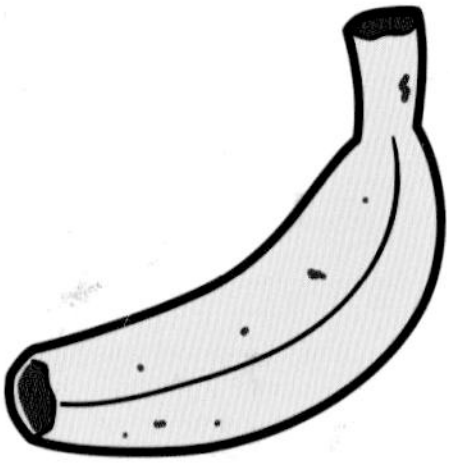

une banane
a banana

une pomme
an apple

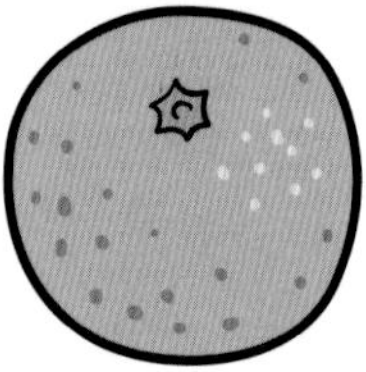

une orange
an orange

Picnic

des chips
some crisps

de l'eau
some water

des raisins
some grapes

un yaourt
a yoghurt

une limonade
a lemonade

Le sport

Quel sport fais-tu?
What sport do you do?

Je joue au tennis.
I play tennis.

Je joue au cricket.
I play cricket.

Je joue au basket.
I play basketball.

Je fais du vélo.
I ride my bike.

Je fais la dance.
I dance.

Je fais de la natation.
I swim.

Je fais du skate.
I skateboard.

Les animaux

J'ai un lapin.
I have a rabbit.

une araignée
a spider

un chien
a dog

un chat
a cat

un poisson rouge
a goldfish

Animals

un hamster

a hamster

un serpent

a snake

un lapin

a rabbit

une souris

a mouse

En ville

Je cherche
une pâtisserie.
I'm looking for
a cake shop.

une boucherie

a butcher

un café

a cafe

une boulangerie

a bakery

une épicerie

a grocer

In town

un fleuriste
a florist

une pâtisserie
a cake shop

une gare
a railway station

un bureau de poste
a post office

Bon anniversaire!

janvier
January

février
February

mars
March

avril
April

mai
May

juin
June

C'est quand, ton anniversaire?
When is your birthday?

Mon anniversaire est en janvier!
My birthday is in January!
J

Happy birthday!

Je mange des bonbons.
I eat some sweets.

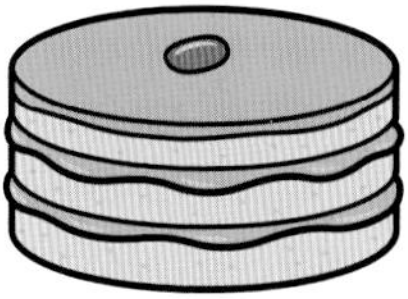

un gâteau
a cake

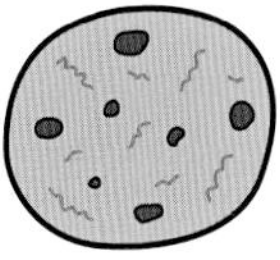

un biscuit
a biscuit

du jus d'orange
some orange juice

J'ai huit ans!
I am 8 years old!

juillet
July

août
August

septembre
September

octobre
October

novembre
November

décembre
December

J'entends un violon.
I hear a violin.

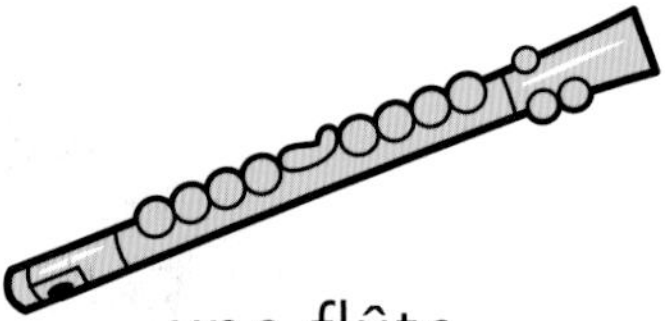

une flûte
a flute

une guitare
a guitar

une flûte à bec
a recorder

un piano
a piano

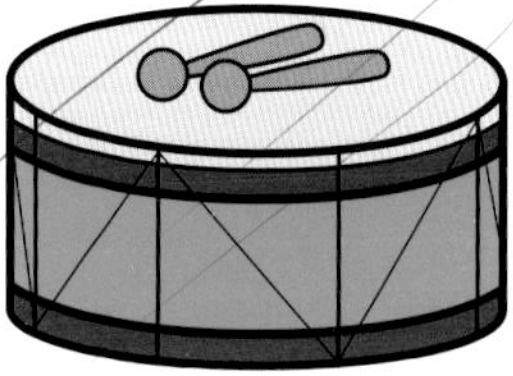

un tambour
a drum

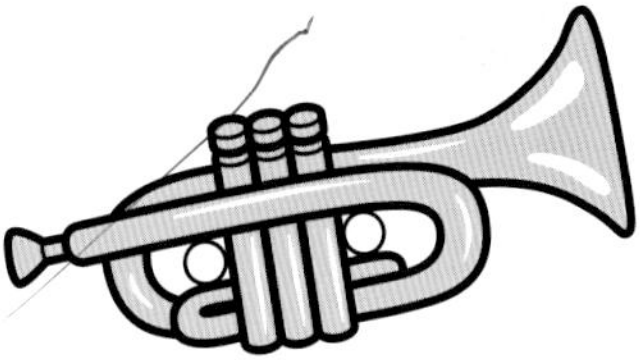

une trompette
a trumpet

un tambourin
a tambourine

un violon
a violin

Incroyable!
Unbelievable!

Mes vêtements

Je porte
un pull bleu.
I'm wearing
a blue jumper.

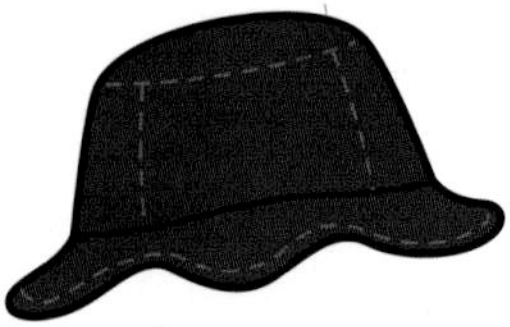

un chapeau noir
a black hat

une jupe orange
an orange skirt

une casquette rouge
a red cap

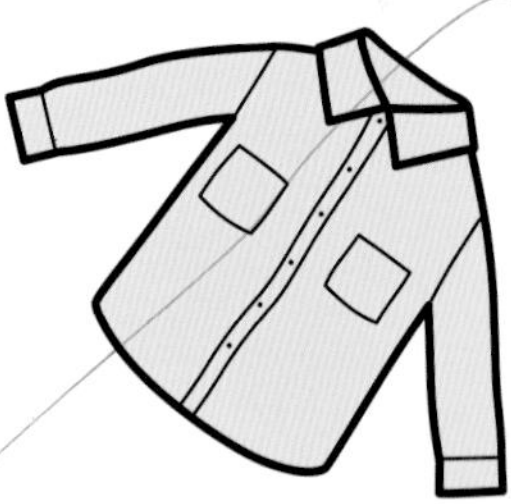

une chemise jaune
a yellow shirt

My clothes

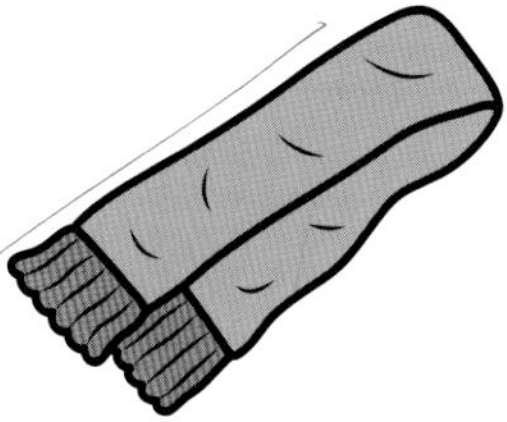

une écharpe rose
a pink scarf

un pull bleu
a blue jumper

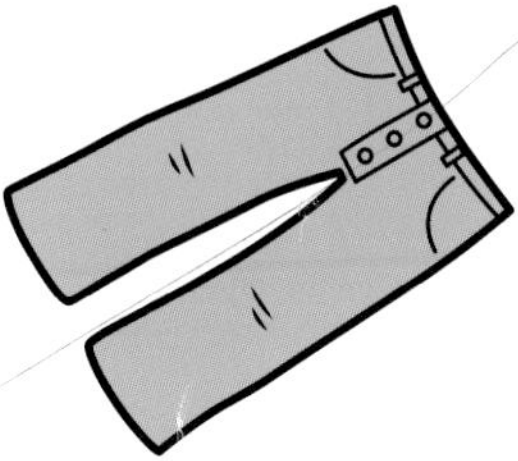

un pantalon vert
a pair of green trousers

un T-shirt blanc
a white T-shirt

Très chic!
Very smart!

- rouge
- orange
- jaune
- vert
- bleu
- noir
- blanc
- rose

Au restaurant

In a restaurant

Menu

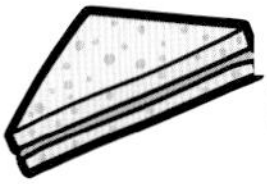

un sandwich au jambon

a ham sandwich

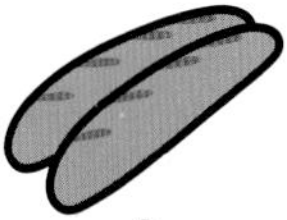

du pain

some bread

un gâteau

a cake

une limonade

a lemonade

un chocolat chaud

a hot chocolate

Informations supplémentaires

Les jours de la semaine
The days of the week

lundi	Monday
mardi	Tuesday
mercredi	Wednesday
jeudi	Thursday
vendredi	Friday
samedi	Saturday
dimanche	Sunday

Les mois de l'année
The months of the year

janvier	January	juillet	July
février	February	août	August
mars	March	septembre	September
avril	April	octobre	October
mai	May	novembre	November
juin	June	décembre	December